HANDS-ON ABCs

ABC Scissor Skills

by Marilynn G. Barr

LAB20142P
Hands-on ABCs
ABC SCISSOR SKILLS
by Marilynn G. Barr

Published by: Little Acorn Books™
Originally published by: Monday Morning Books, Inc.

Entire contents copyright © 2014 Little Acorn Books™

Little Acorn Books
PO Box 8787
Greensboro, NC 27419-0787

Promoting Early Skills for a Lifetime™

Little Acorn Books™
is an imprint of Little Acorn Associates, Inc.

http://www.littleacornbooks.com

Permission is hereby granted to reproduce student materials in this book for non-commercial individual or classroom use. *School-wide or system-wide use is expressly prohibited.

ISBN 978-1-937257-58-3

Printed in the United States of America

ABC Scissor Skills Contents

Introduction 4	Mitten 33
Matching Alphabet Pictures 5	Letter Mm and Pictures 34
Alphabet Shape Books 5	Nest 35
Textured Alphabets 6	Letter Nn and Pictures 36
Counting Alphabet Pictures 6	Owl 37
My Alphabet Picture Book 7	Letter Oo and Pictures 38
My Alphabet Portfolio 7	Pocket 39
Alphabet Writing Book 8	Letter Pp and Pictures 40
Writing Practice Shape Booklets 8	Quilt 41
Apron 9	Letter Qq and Pictures 42
Letter Aa and Pictures 10	Rabbit 43
Bear 11	Letter Rr and Pictures 44
Letter Bb and Pictures 12	Snowman 45
Cat 13	Letter Ss and Pictures 46
Letter Cc and Pictures 14	Tree 47
Dog 15	Letter Tt and Pictures 48
Letter Dd and Pictures 16	Umbrella 49
Egg 17	Letter Uu and Pictures 50
Letter Ee and Pictures 18	Vest 51
Fish 19	Letter Vv and Pictures 52
Letter Ff and Pictures 20	Whale 53
Ghost 21	Letter Ww and Pictures 54
Letter Gg and Pictures 22	A Giant X 55
Hippopotamus 23	Letter Xx and Pictures 56
Letter Hh and Pictures 24	Yo-yo 57
Igloo 25	Letter Yy and Pictures 58
Letter Ii and Pictures 26	Zebra 59
Jar 27	Letter Zz and Pictures 60
Letter Jj and Pictures 28	More Alphabet Pictures 61
Koala 29	My Alphabet Portfolio Cover 64
Letter Kk and Pictures 30	
Ladybug 31	
Letter Ll and Pictures 32	

ABC Scissor Skills Introduction

ABC Scissor Skills is one of four Hands-on ABC books (**ABC Art, ABC Mini Books,** and **ABC Games**) designed to provide alphabet skills practice for early learners. Children practice recognizing letters and letter sounds and associating letters with alphabet pictures while developing fine motor skills such as coloring, cutting, and gluing. Activities also offer sorting, counting, sequencing, and writing skills practice while fostering individual creativity.

Reproduce the patterns on pages 9-60 for children to make Matching Alphabet Pictures, Alphabet Shape Books, Textured Alphabets, Alphabet Picture Books, and Alphabet Portfolios. Patterns include a large alphabet picture pattern, alphabet picture squares, a letter tracing medallion, and an upper- and lowercase letter for each letter of the alphabet. Additional alphabet picture squares can be found on pages 61-63.

Prepare a workstation with the materials listed here for a creative alphabet skills practice center.

Materials List

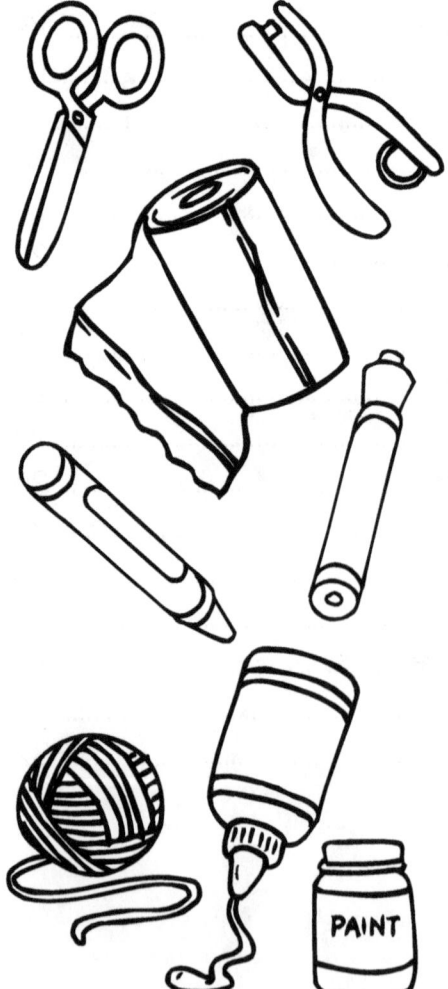

- construction paper
- oak tag
- folders
- crayons
- markers
- scissors
- finger-painting paper
- finger paints
- craft sticks
- wallpaper scraps
- pom poms
- glitter
- cotton balls
- beads
- beans
- yarn
- elbow macaroni (uncooked)
- rice (uncooked)
- popcorn (popped and unpopped)
- buttons
- glue
- stapler

Matching Alphabet Pictures

Reproduce a construction paper alphabet picture pattern and matching alphabet picture and letter squares for each child to color and cut out. Have children glue the matching letter squares to their alphabet picture patterns. Then have them glue one set of matching picture squares on the alphabet picture. Alternate the activity by having the children glue assorted picture squares onto their alphabet picture patterns. Write each child's name on the front of his or her alphabet picture. Mount finished pictures on a display board entitled We Know Our Alphabet.

Alphabet Shape Books

Reproduce six identical oak tag alphabet picture patterns for each child. Have children color and cut out each pattern. Reproduce matching medallion, letter, and picture squares for children to color, cut out, and glue onto alphabet pictures. Have children decorate one pattern to use as a cover for their Alphabet Shape Books. Then help each child write A Book About (letter) on the cover. Have children trace the letters, then glue the matching medallion onto one pattern, cutout letter squares onto another pattern, and each set of matching picture squares onto the remaining patterns. Punch a hole at the top of each child's set of patterns. Stack the patterns with the cover on top and insert and secure a brass fastener through the holes to form an Alphabet Shape Book.

Textured Alphabets

Reproduce an oak tag alphabet picture pattern for each child. Prepare a work station with materials listed below for children to create Textured Alphabets. Have children color and cut out their patterns. Then demonstrate how to apply glue and attach materials such as cottons balls, beads, or beans onto a pattern. Write each child's name on the front of the finished projects. Post finished projects on a display board entitled Our Textured Alphabets.

Texture Materials

cotton balls	beans
beads	sequins
sand	buttons
pom poms	bird seed
felt scraps	yarn
cereal O's	uncooked pasta
fish crackers	bubble wrap scraps
small stones	unpopped popcorn
small artificial flowers	popped popcorn
plastic fishing worms	

Counting Alphabet Pictures

Reproduce a construction paper alphabet picture pattern for each child to color and cut out. Also reproduce two sets of matching picture squares (for example: two sets of apple squares). Call out a number and have children glue the matching number of picture squares onto their cut-out patterns. Then help each child write the correct numeral on his or her pattern. Write each child's name on the front of his or her alphabet picture. Mount finished pictures on a display board entitled Counting Alphabet Pictures.

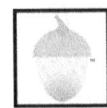
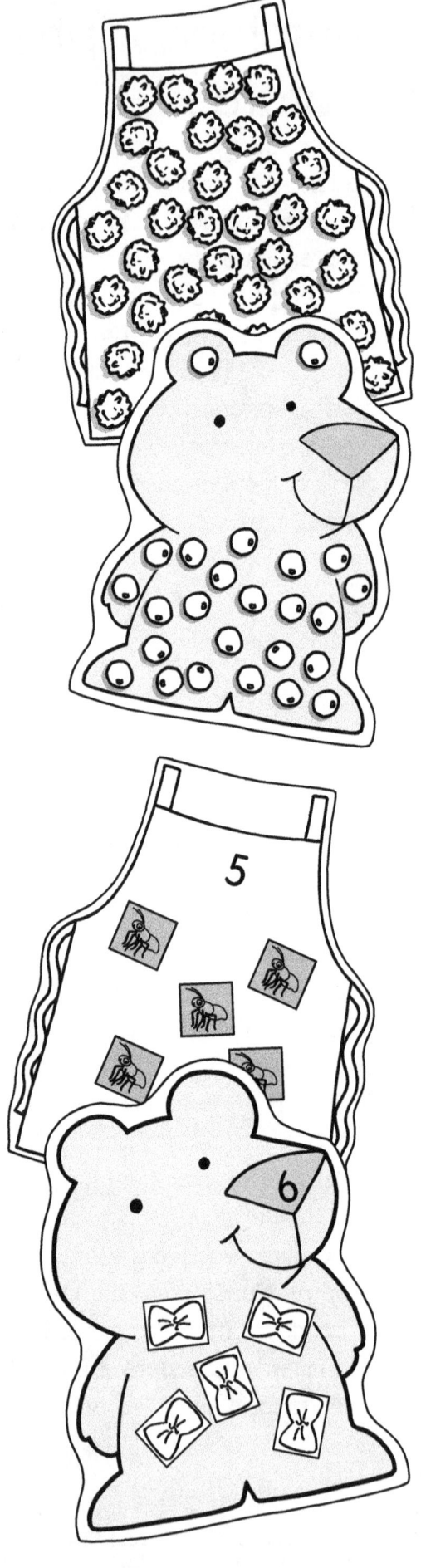

My Alphabet Picture Book

Reproduce construction paper alphabet picture patterns for each child to color and cut out. Help each child write the matching upper- and lowercase letters and word on their cut-out patterns. Provide 26 sheets of construction paper for each child. Have children glue each cut-out pattern onto a separate sheet of construction paper. Then provide each child with a large sheet of construction paper to fold in half and decorate to use as a cover. Help children write My Alphabet Picture Book on their covers. Write each child's name on the front of his or her book.

My Alphabet Portfolio

Provide each child with a large sheet of oak tag. Help each child fold his or her oak tag sheet in half to form a portfolio. Reproduce two portfolio patterns (p. 64) for each child to color and cut out. Have children glue their portfolio patterns onto each side of their oak tag portfolios. Punch two holes along the wide edges of each child's portfolio as shown here. Measure, cut, and lace two lengths of yarn to thread and tie to each side of the portfolio. Help each child write his or her name on each portfolio pattern. Children can store their alphabet pictures and shape books in their portfolios. Writing practice sheets and alphabet activity sheets can also be stored in portfolios. Display children's portfolios filled with work during open house.

Alphabet Writing Book

Make an Alphabet Writing book for children to practice writing the alphabet. Reproduce, color, cut out, and glue alphabet picture patterns onto separate sheets of construction paper. Reproduce, color, cut out, and glue the matching medallions onto each pattern. Laminate each page. Fold, then decorate a large sheet of oak tag for a cover. Write Alphabet Writing on the cover. Stack the pages in alphabetical order, insert them inside the cover, then staple to form a book. Provide wipe-off crayons or markers for children to practice tracing.

Writing Practice Shape Booklets

Provide materials for children to make Writing Practice Shape Booklets. Program one alphabet picture pattern with one or more manuscript writing lines. Reproduce eleven identical construction paper patterns for each child to color and cut out. Have children decorate a cutout to use as a cover. Help each child write his or her name on the cover. Stack then punch a hole at the top of each child's set of cutouts with the cover on top. Insert and secure a brass fastener through the holes to form a writing practice booklet. Children can practice writing individual letters and their names.

Apron

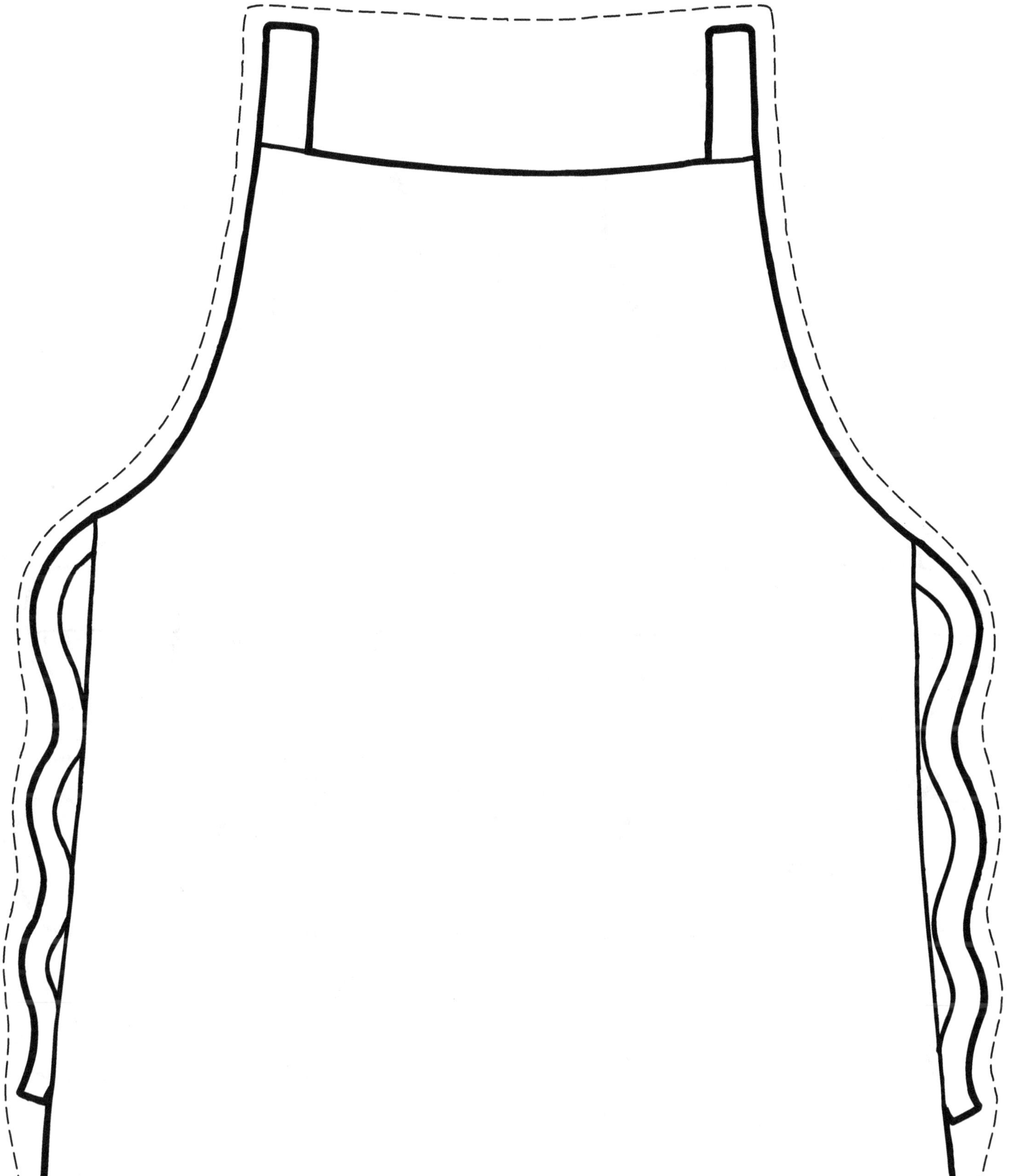
LAB20142 • ABC SCISSOR SKILLS • 978-1-937257-58-3 • © 2014 Little Acorn Books™

Letter Aa and Pictures

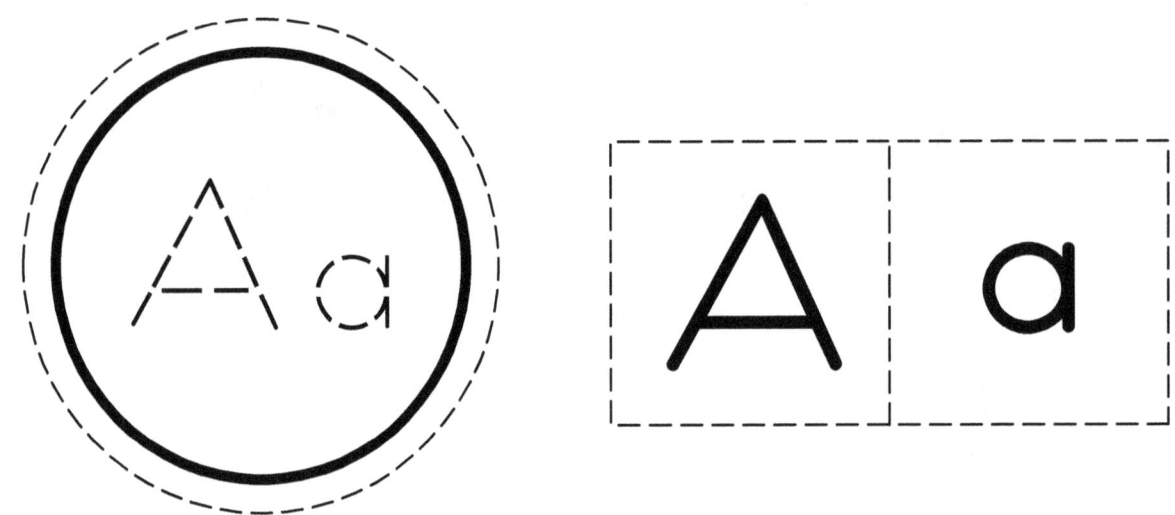

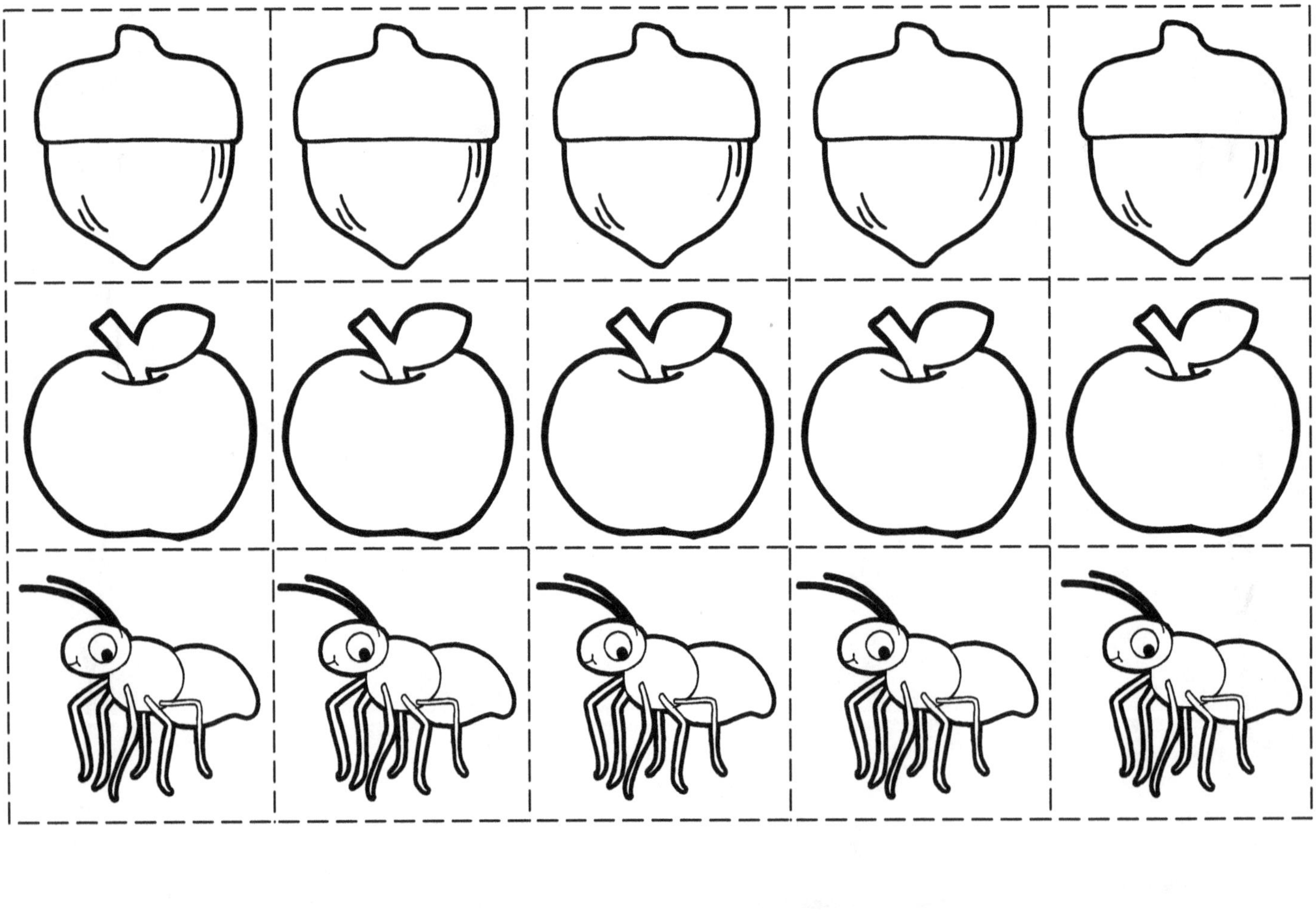

Bear

Letter Bb and Pictures

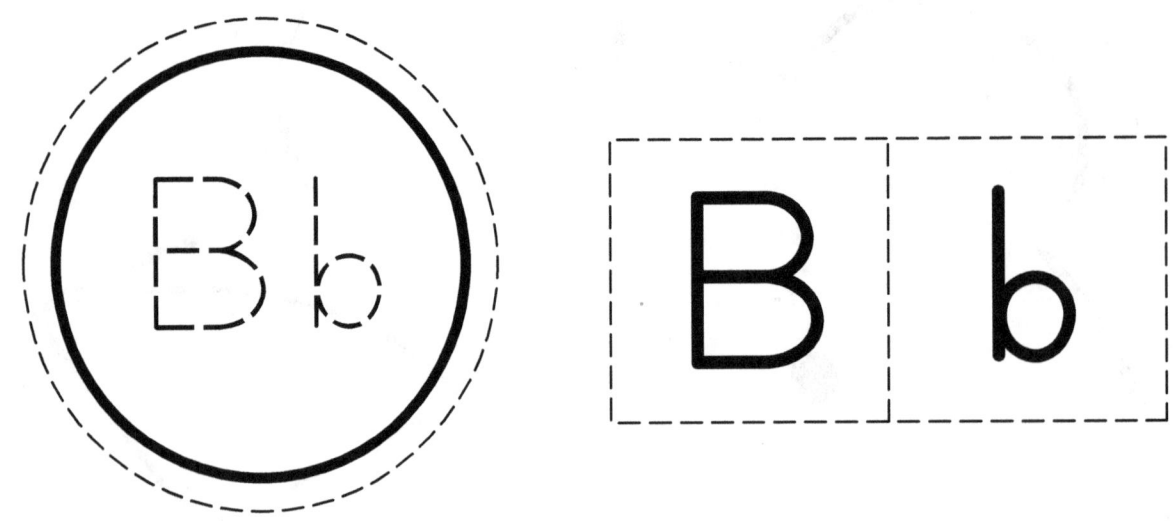

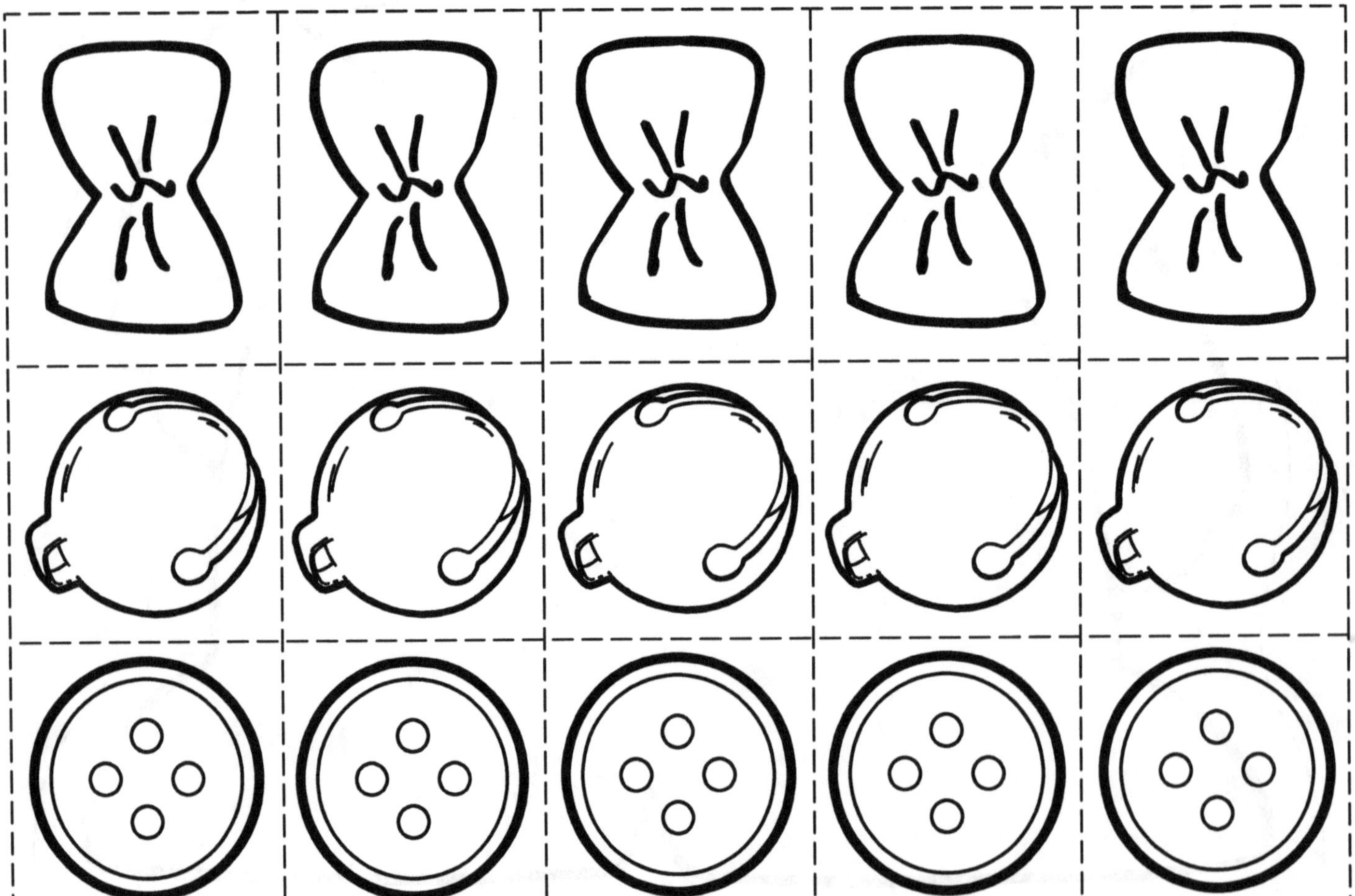

Cat

Letter Cc and Pictures

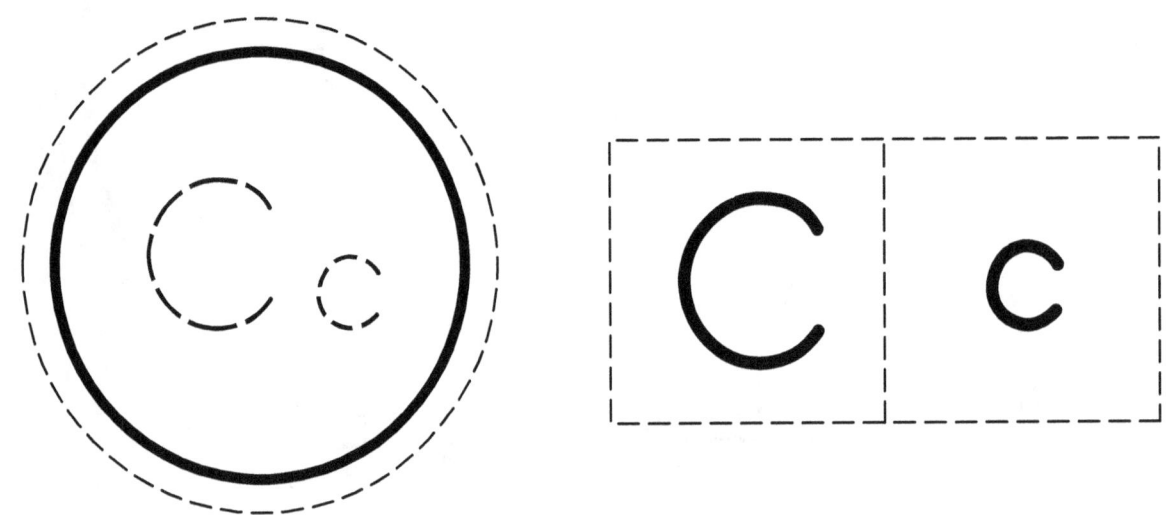

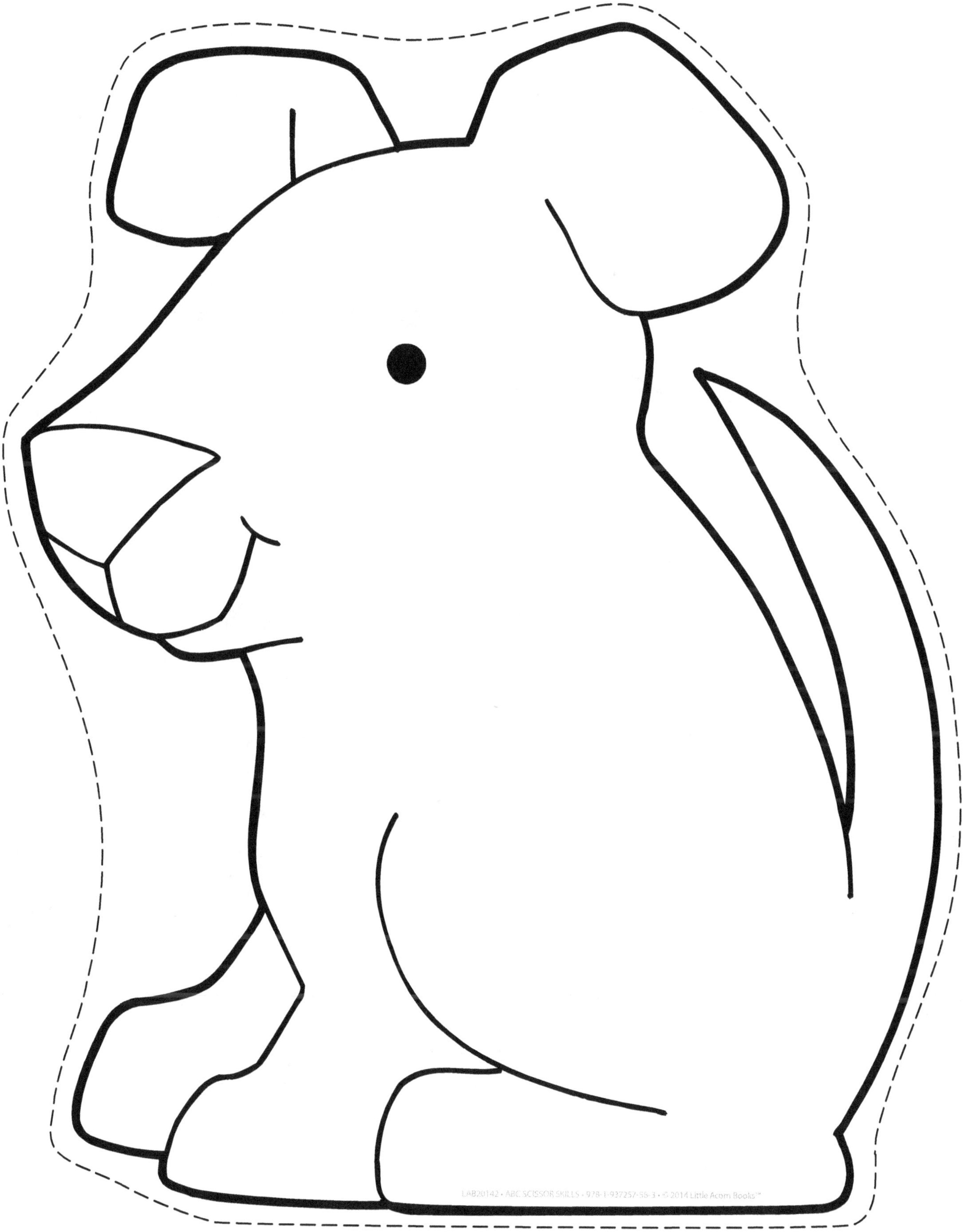
LAB20142 • ABC SCISSOR SKILLS • 978-1-937257-58-3 • © 2014 Little Acorn Books™

Letter Dd and Pictures

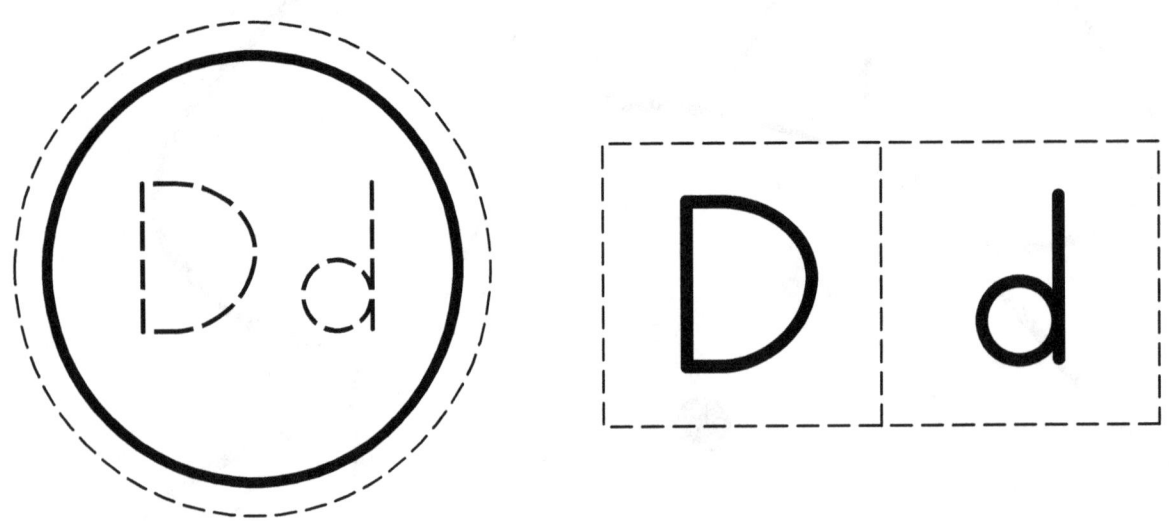

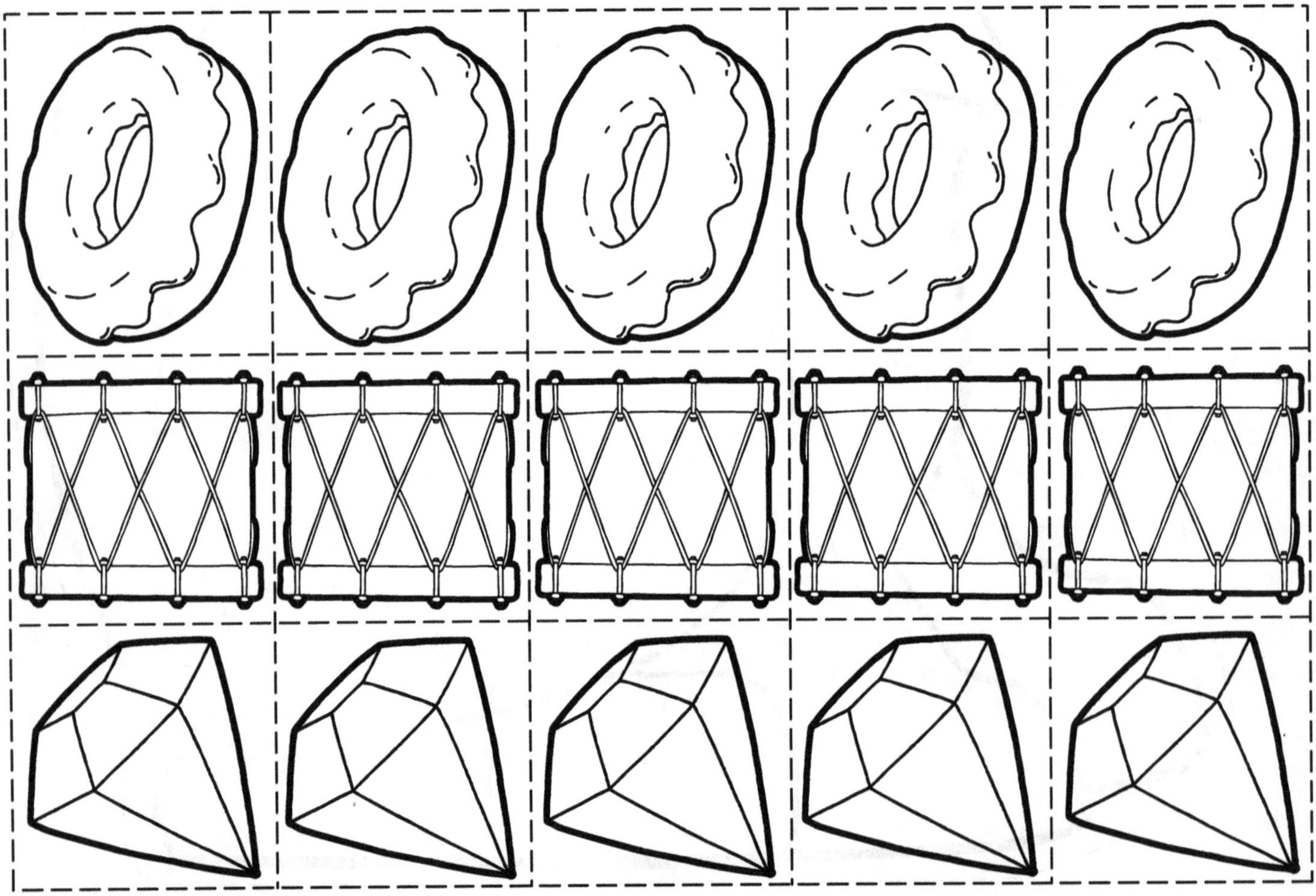

Egg

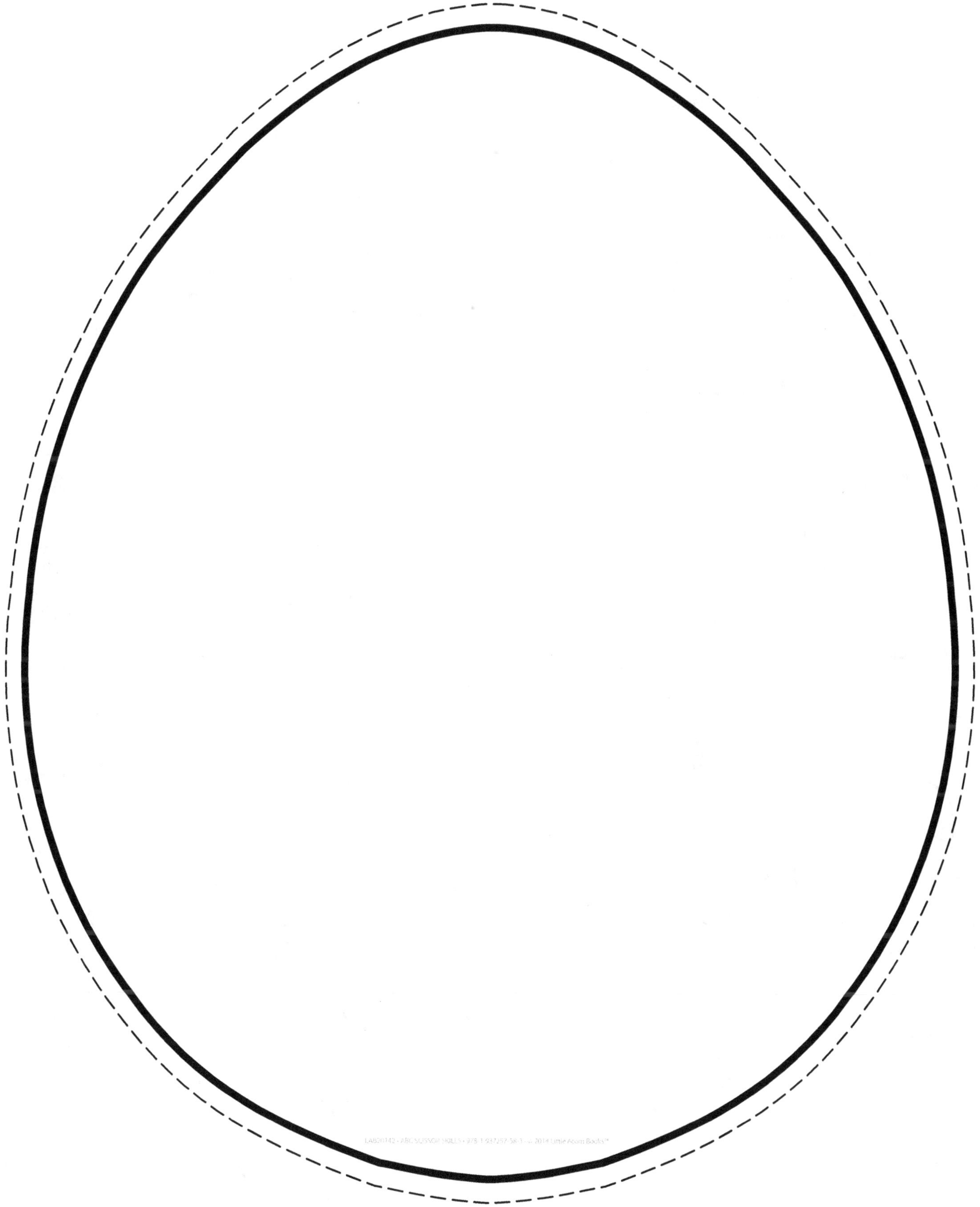

Letter Ee and Pictures

E e

E e

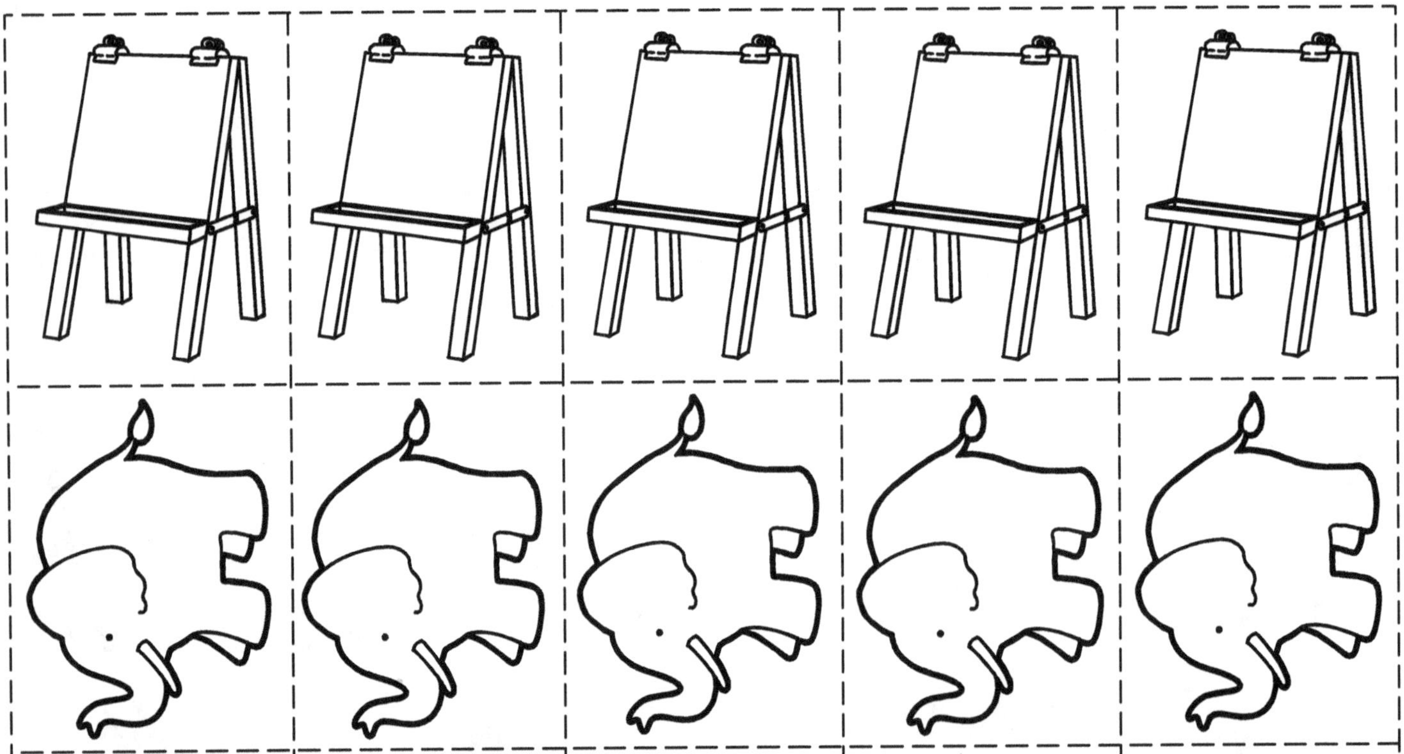

8 8 8 8 8

LAB20142P • ABC SCISSOR SKILLS • 978-1-937257-58-3 • © 2014 Little Acorn Books™

Fish

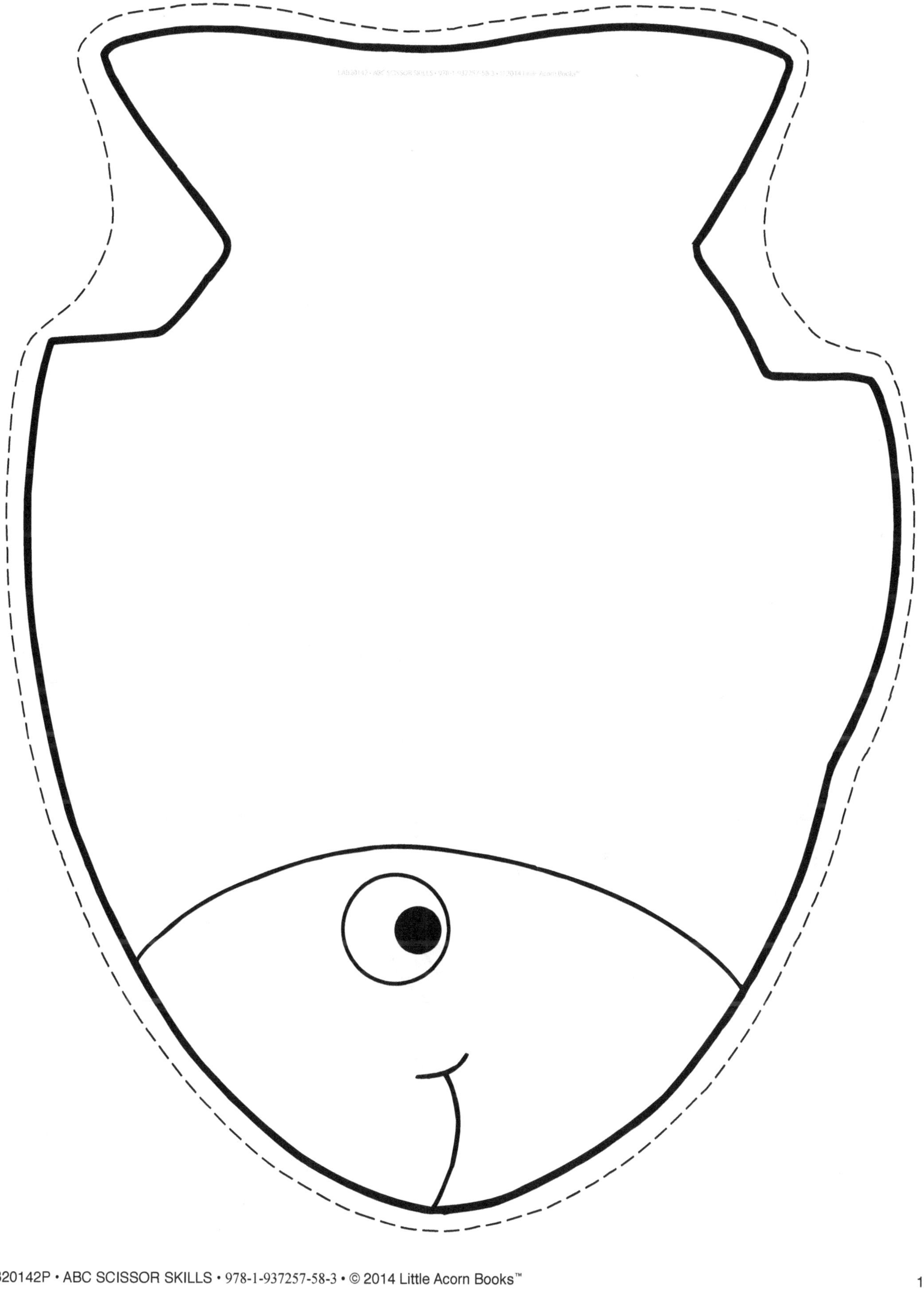

Letter Ff and Pictures

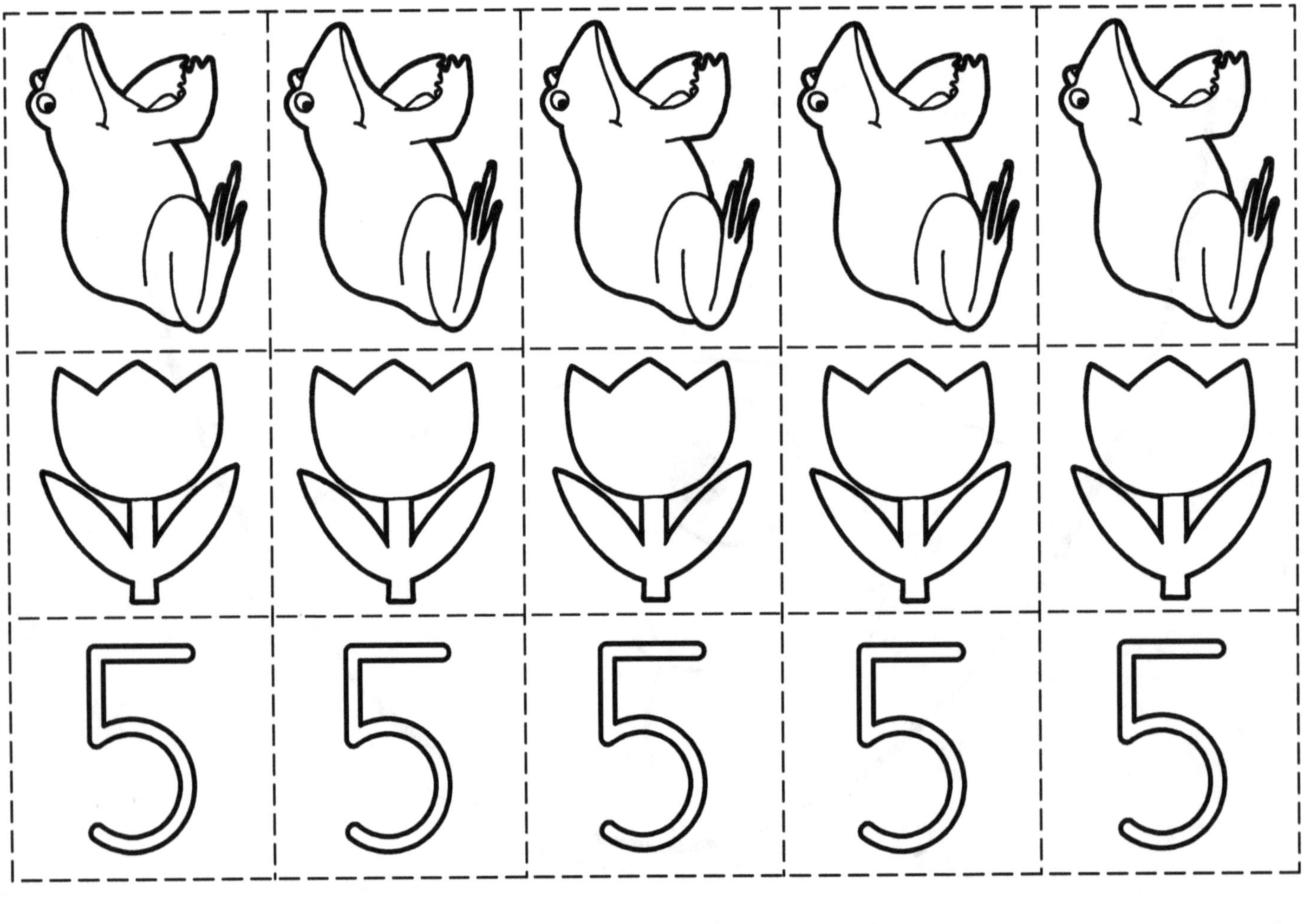

Ghost

Letter Gg and Pictures

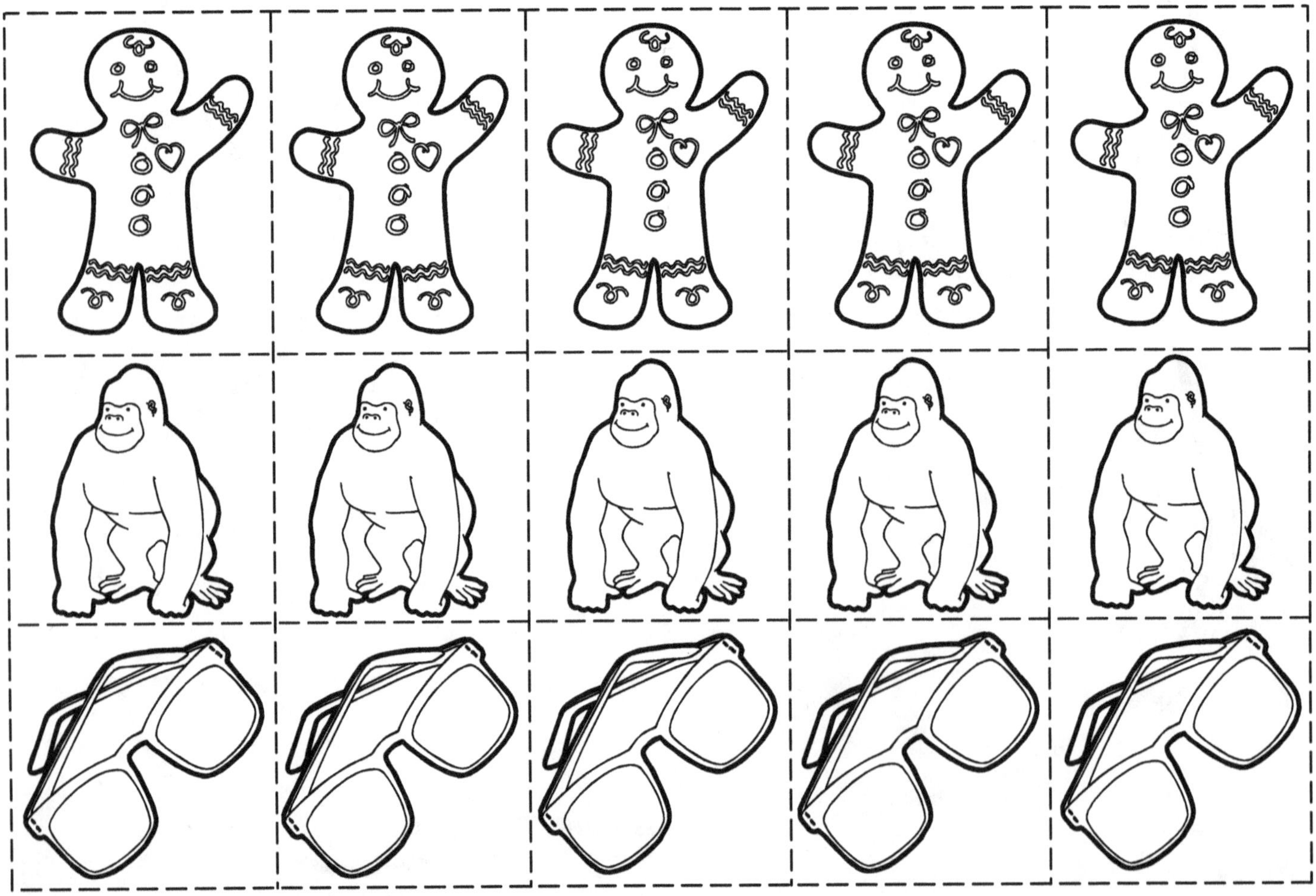

Hippopotamus

Letter Hh and Pictures

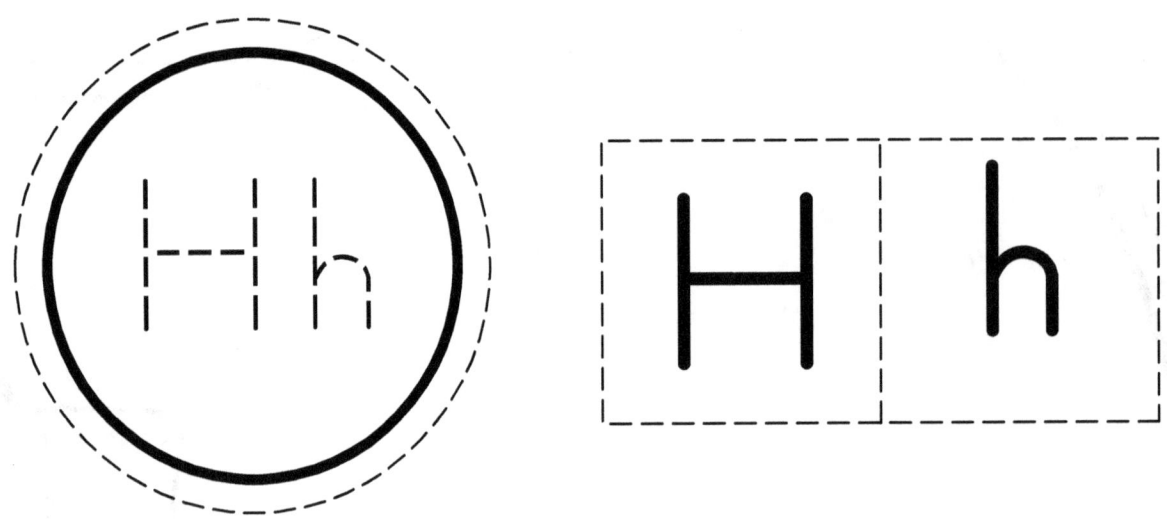

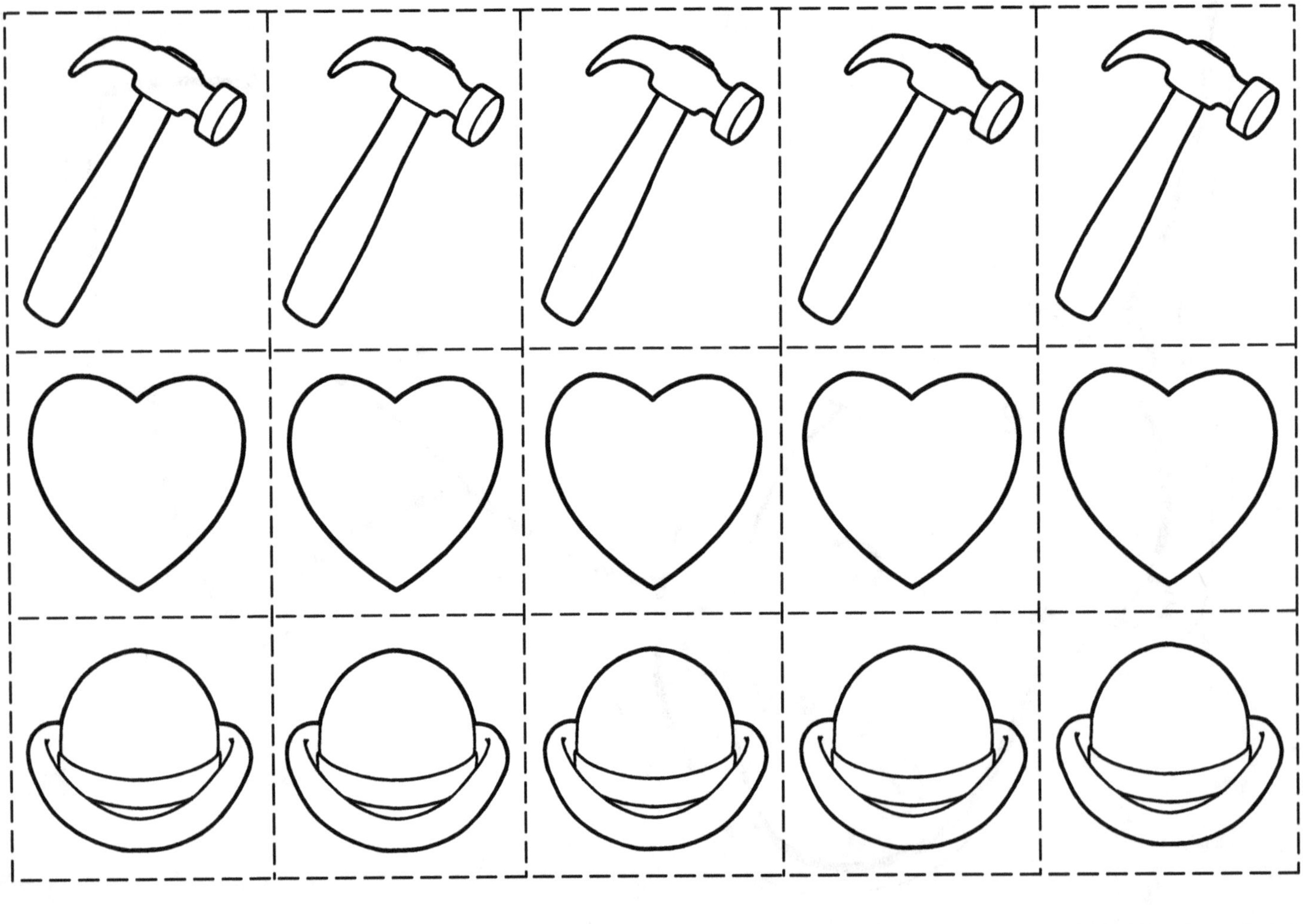

Igloo

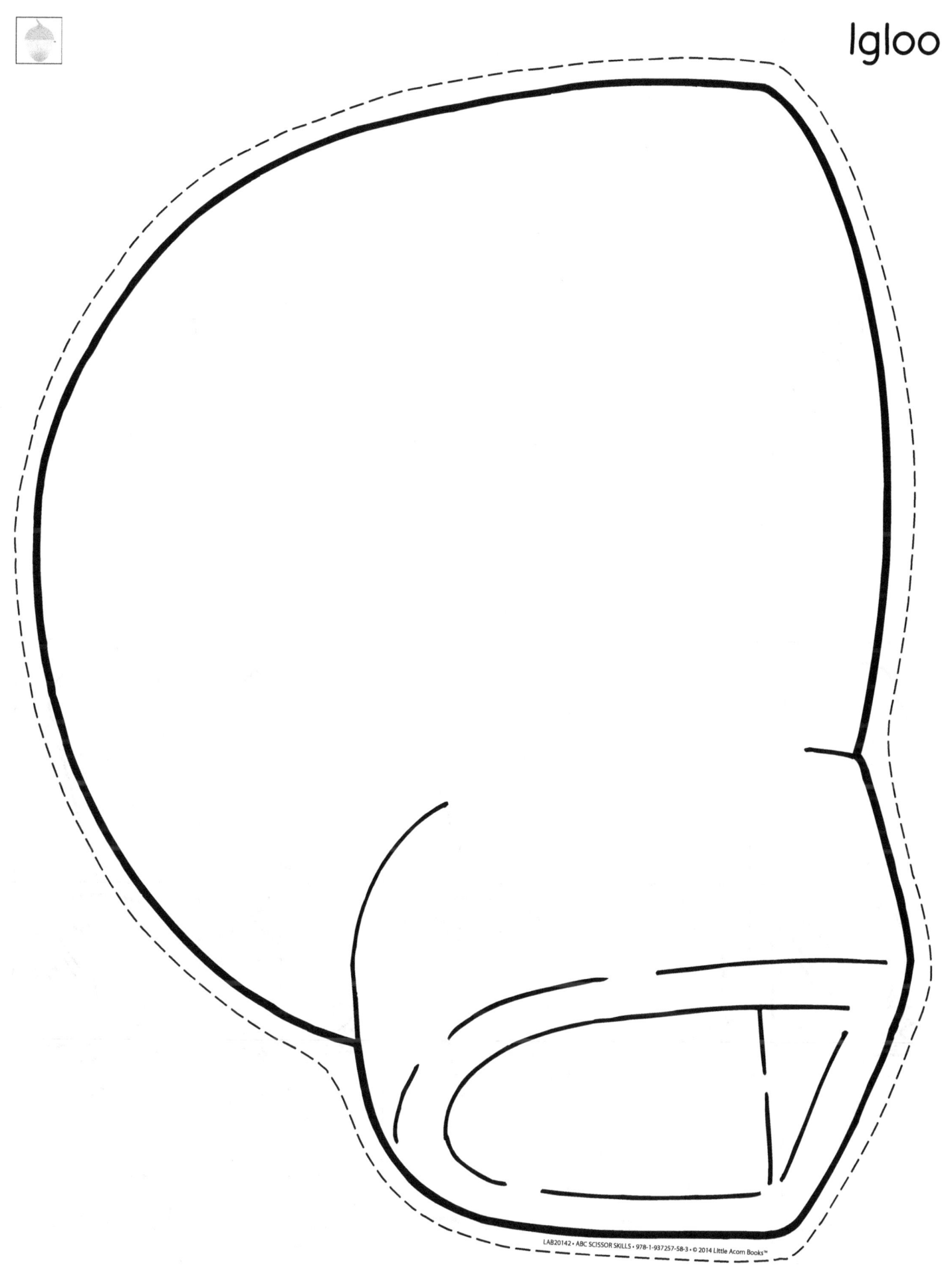

Letter Ii and Pictures

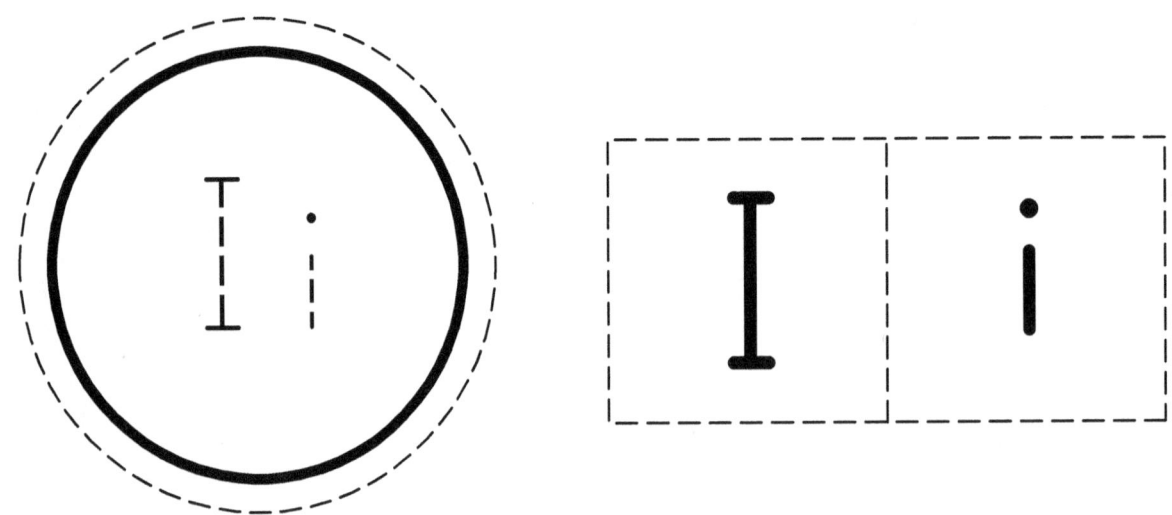

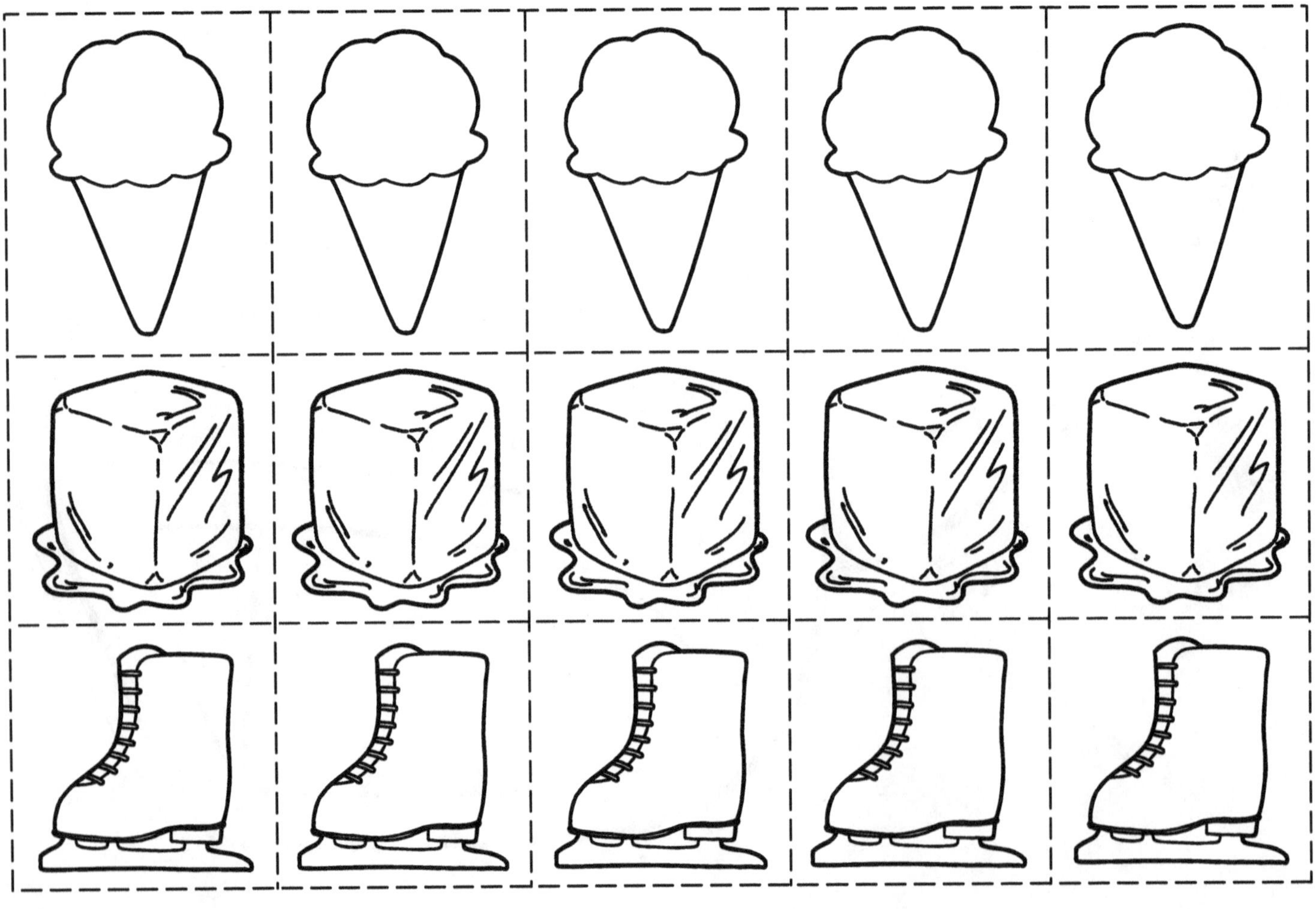

Jar

Letter Jj and Pictures

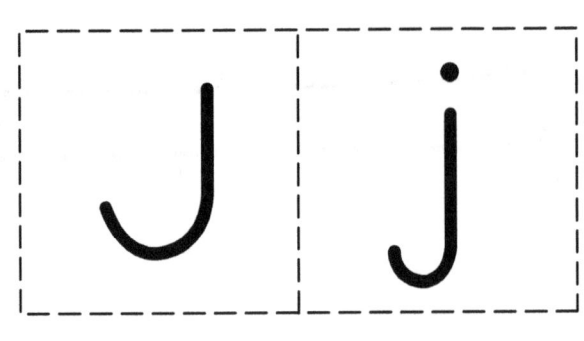

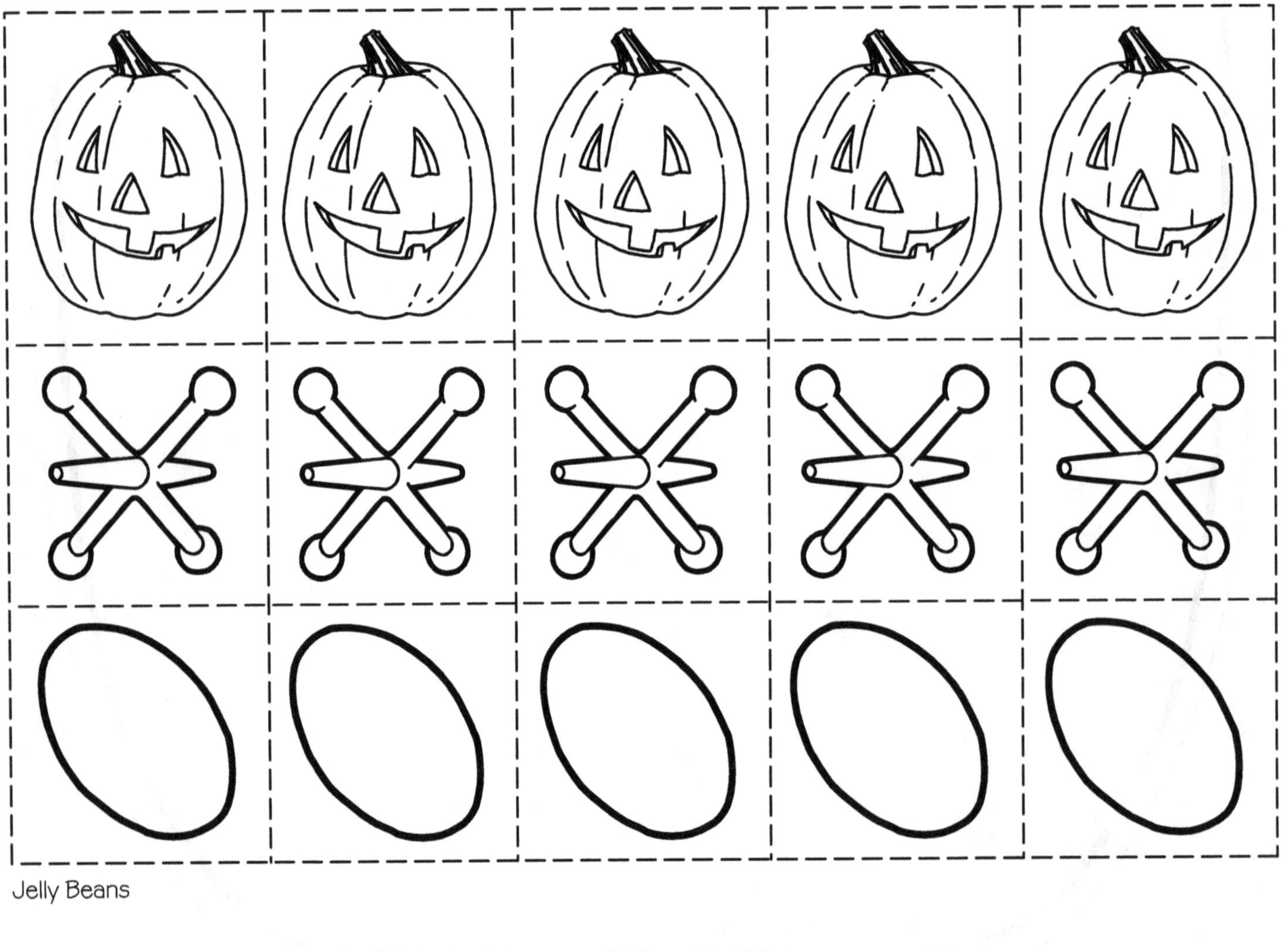

Jelly Beans

Koala

Letter Kk and Pictures

Kk

K k

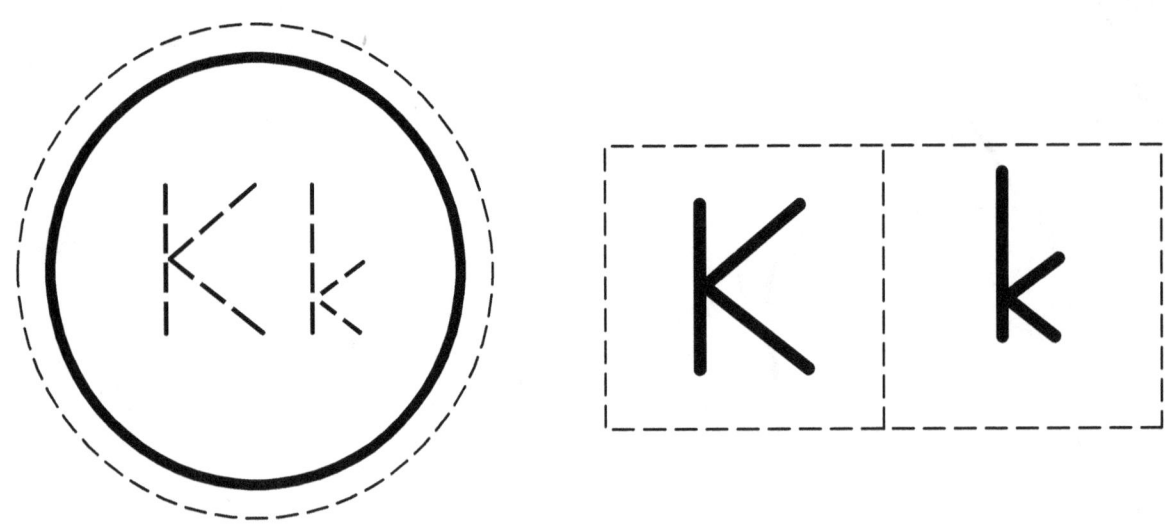

kettle
kettle
kettle
kettle
kettle

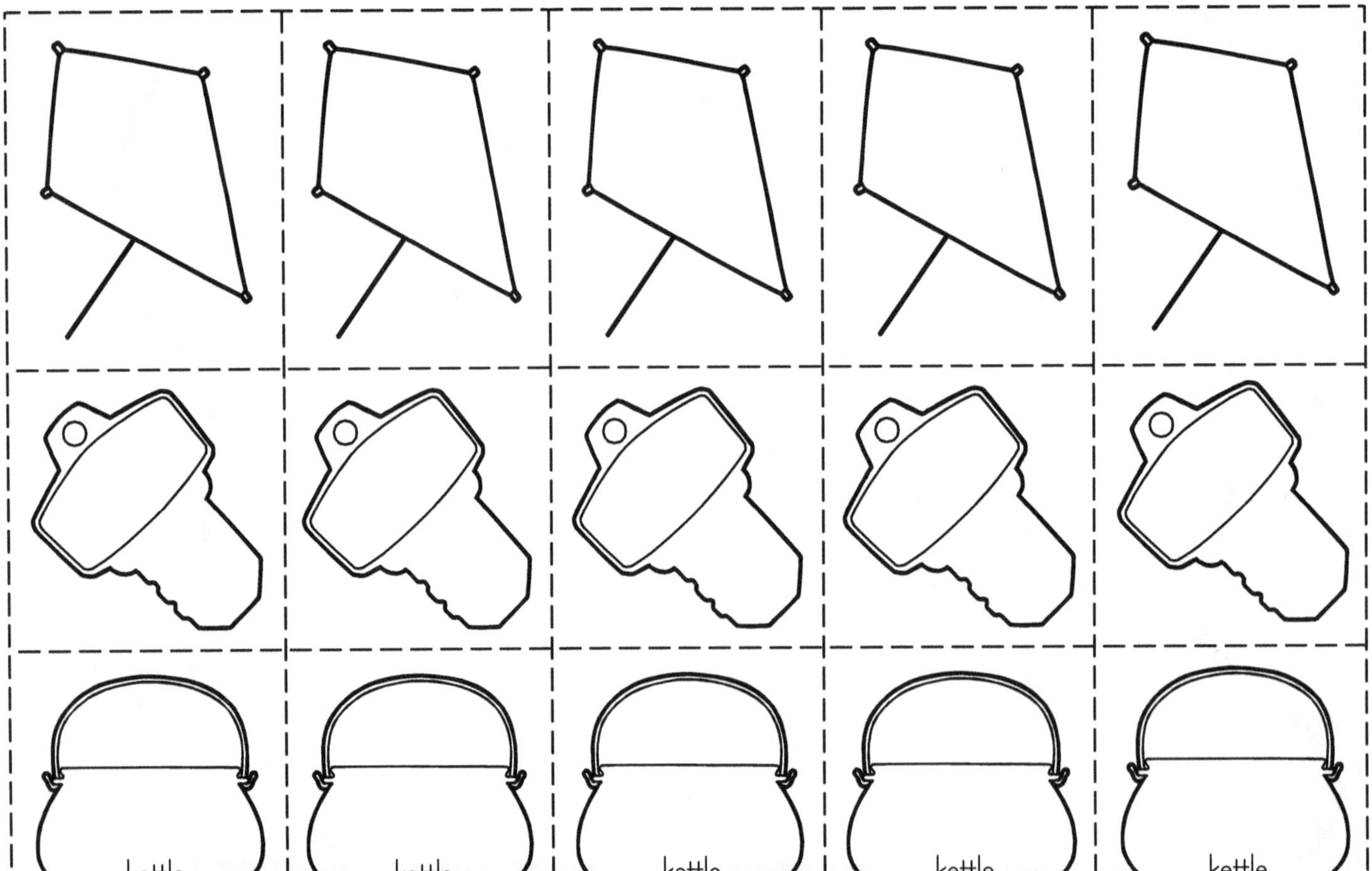

Ladybug

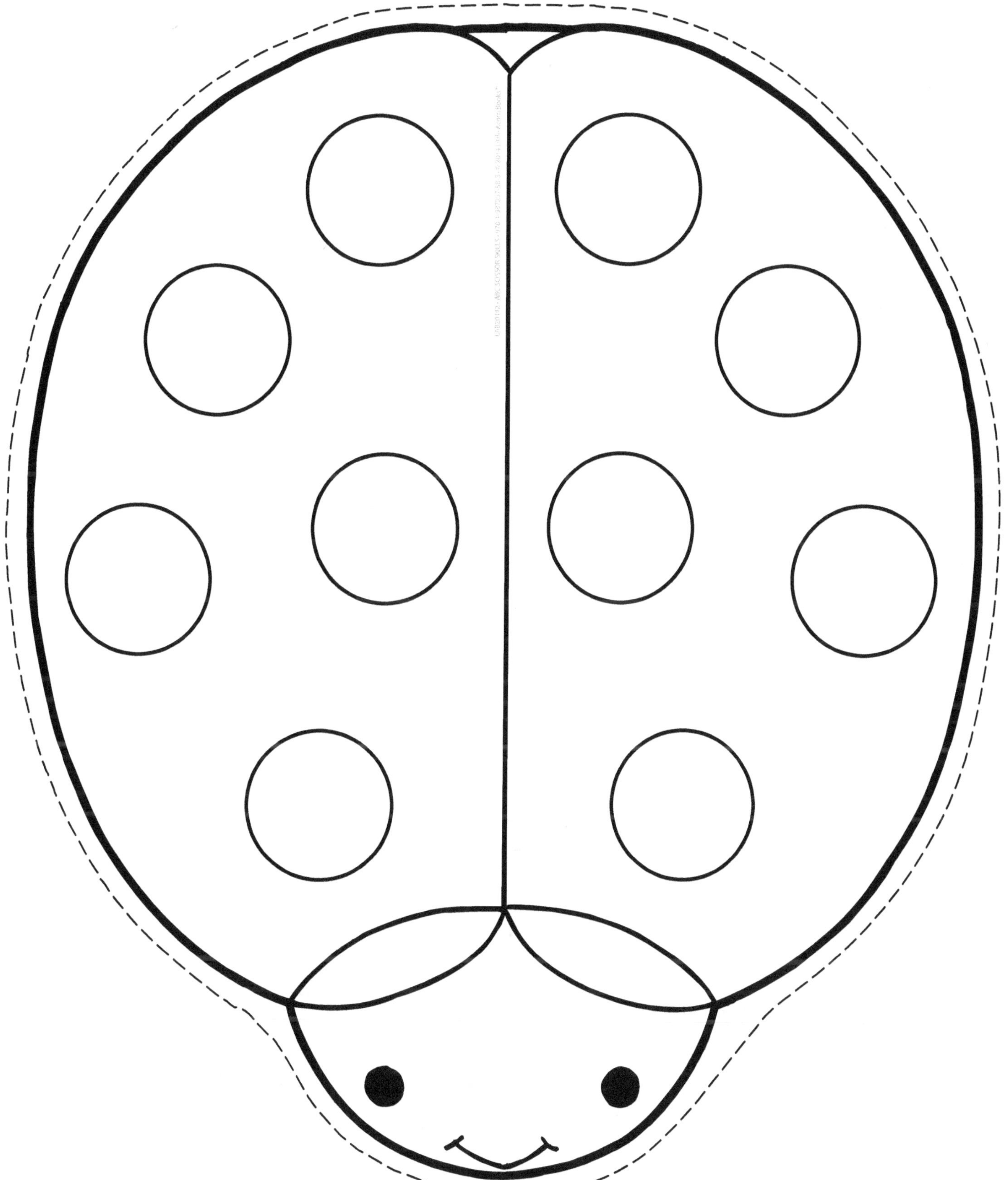

Letter Ll and Pictures

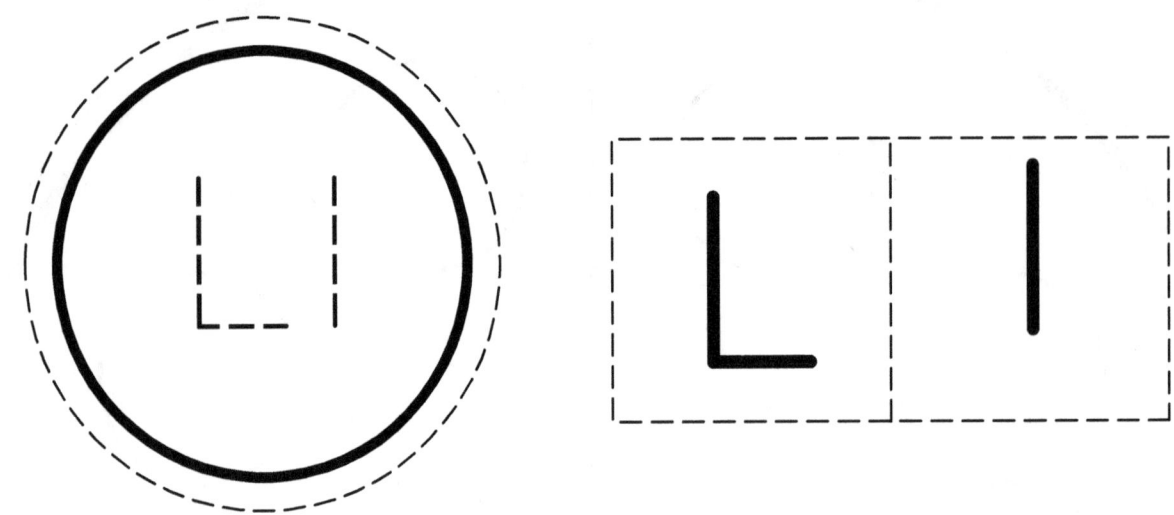

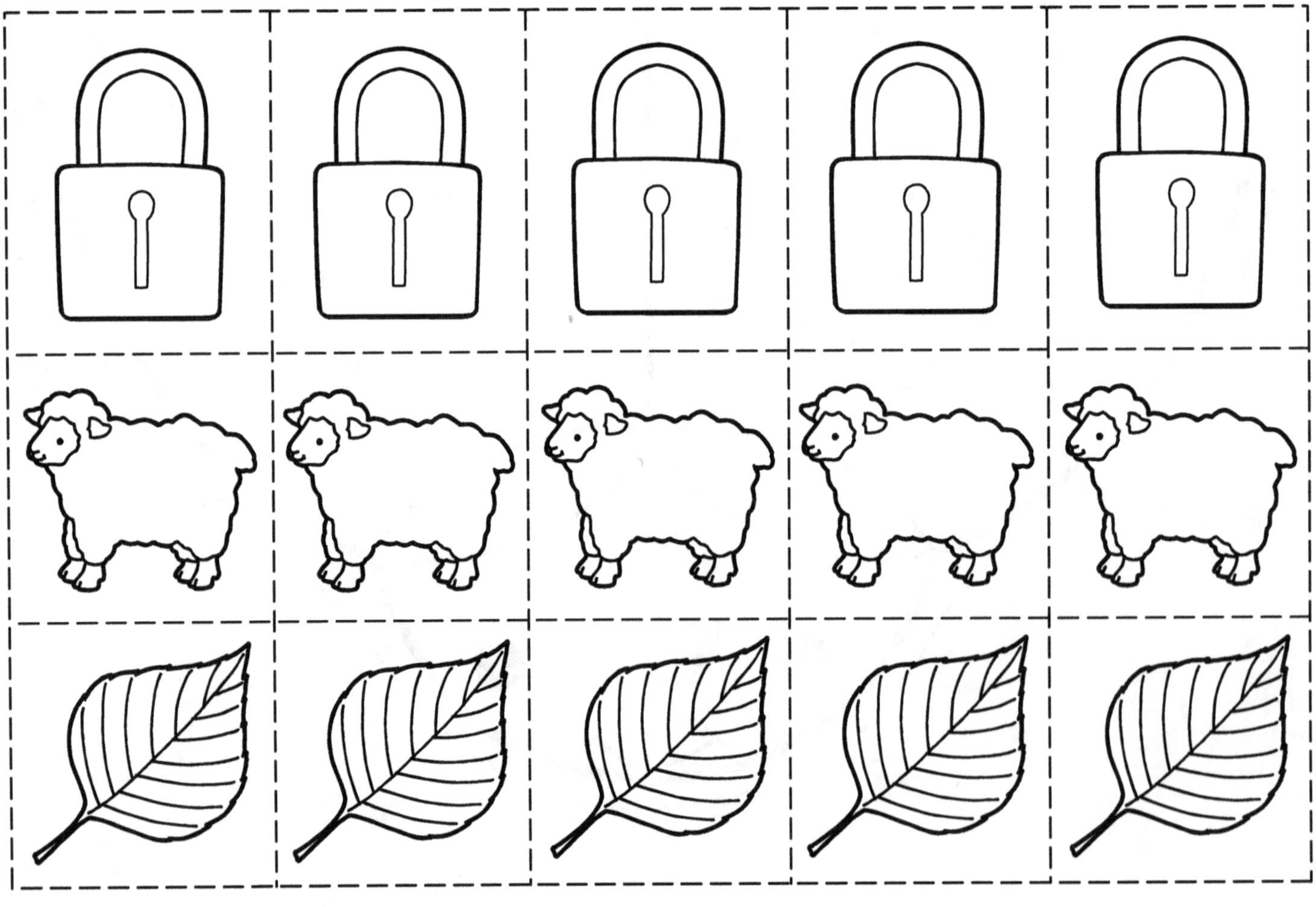

Mitten

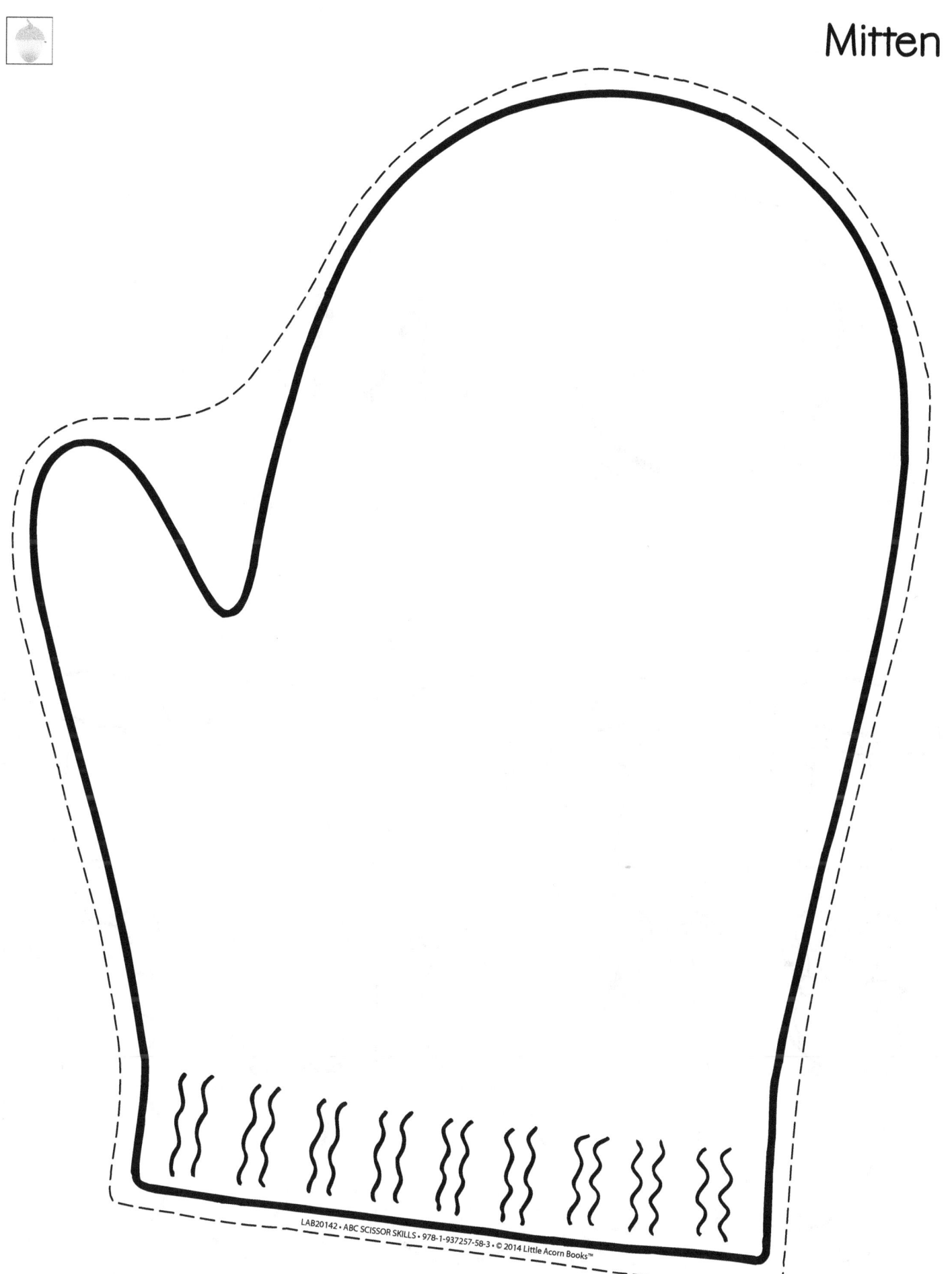

Letter Mm and Pictures

Mm

M m

LAB20142P • ABC SCISSOR SKILLS • 978-1-937257-58-3 • © 2014 Little Acorn Books™

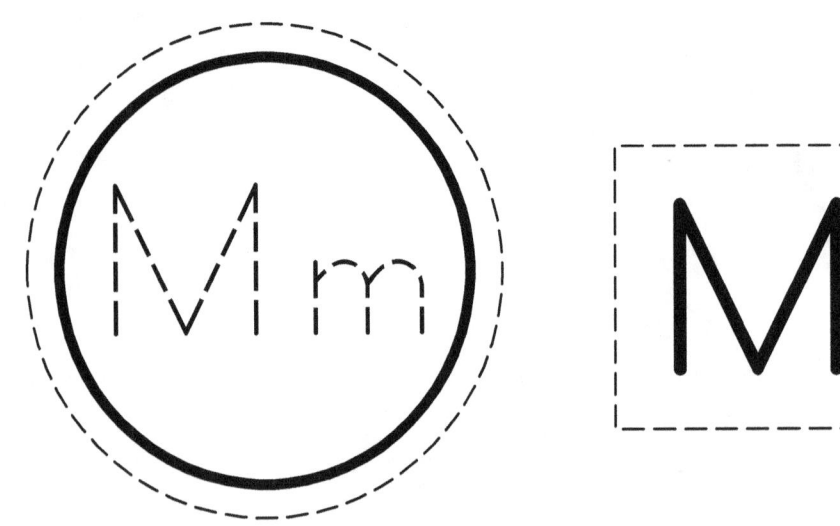

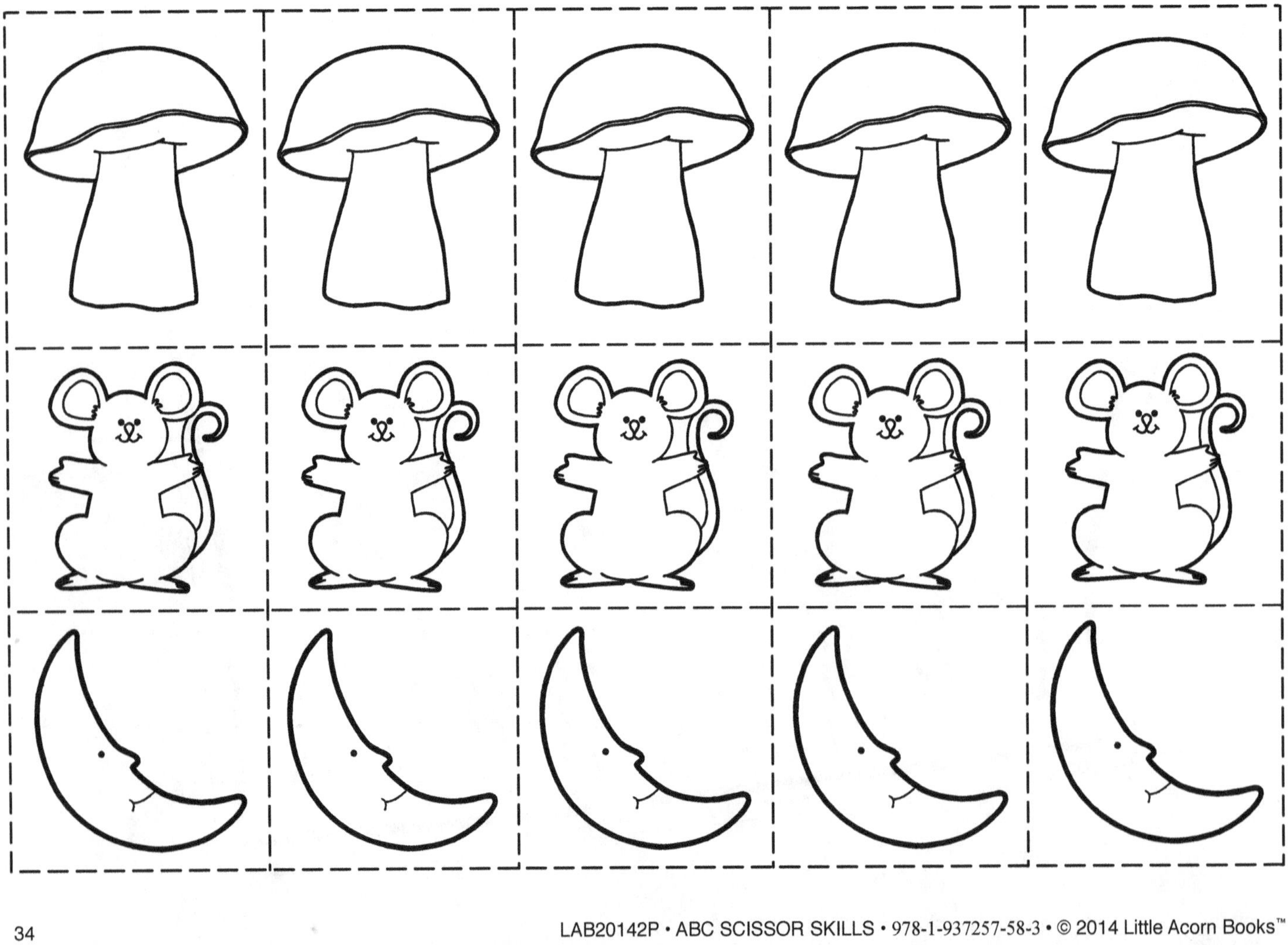

Nest

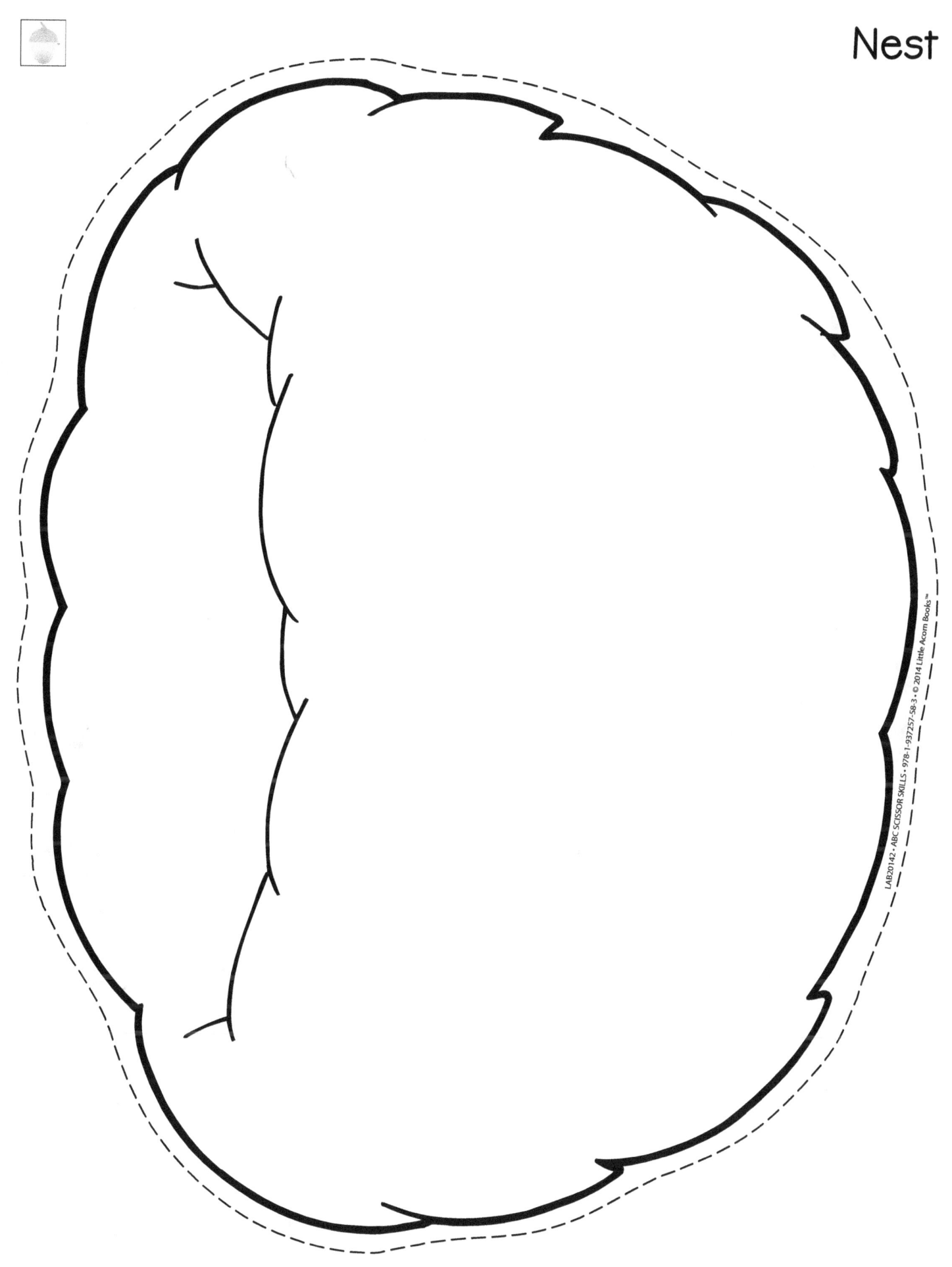

Letter Nn and Pictures

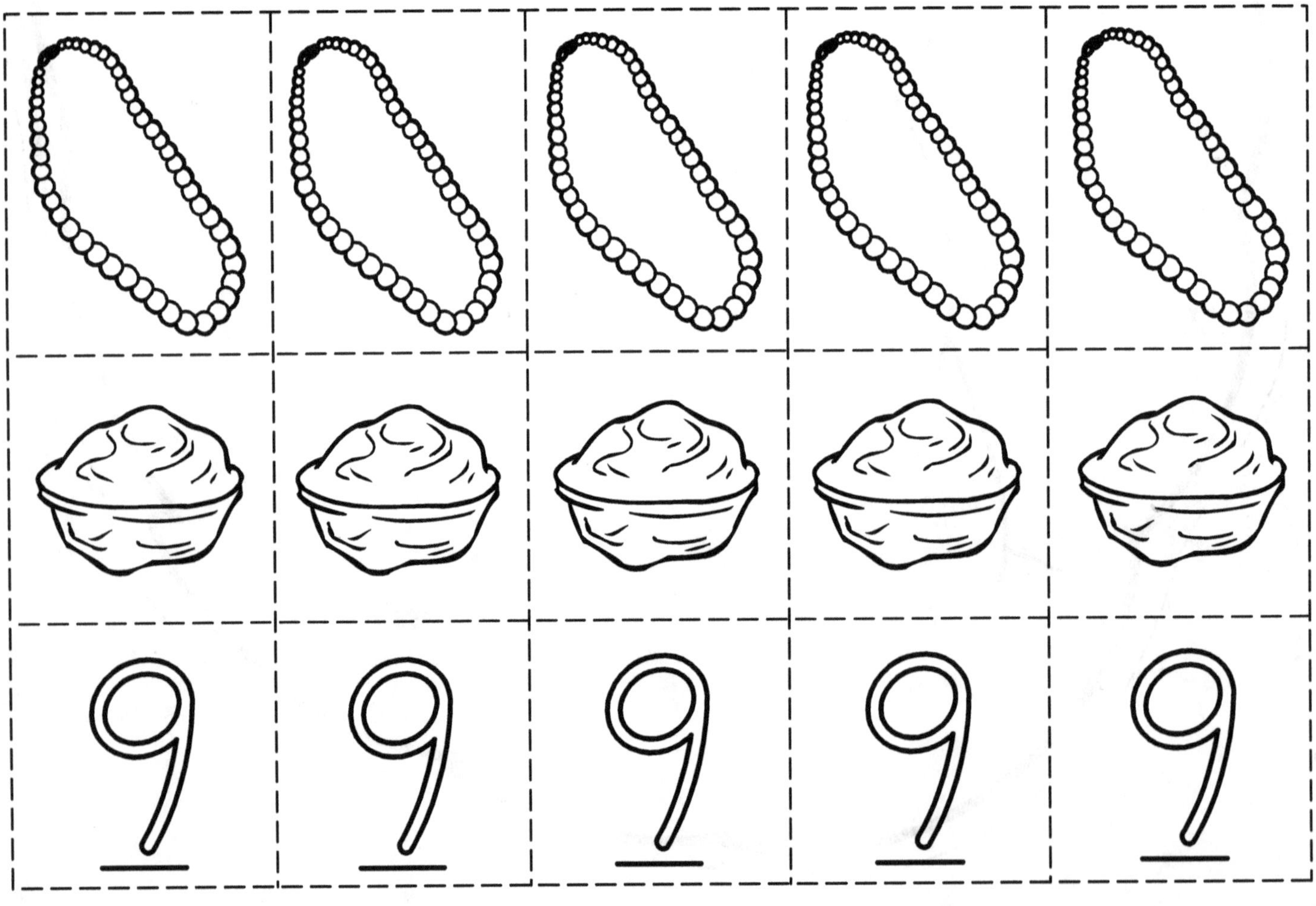

Owl

Letter Oo and Pictures

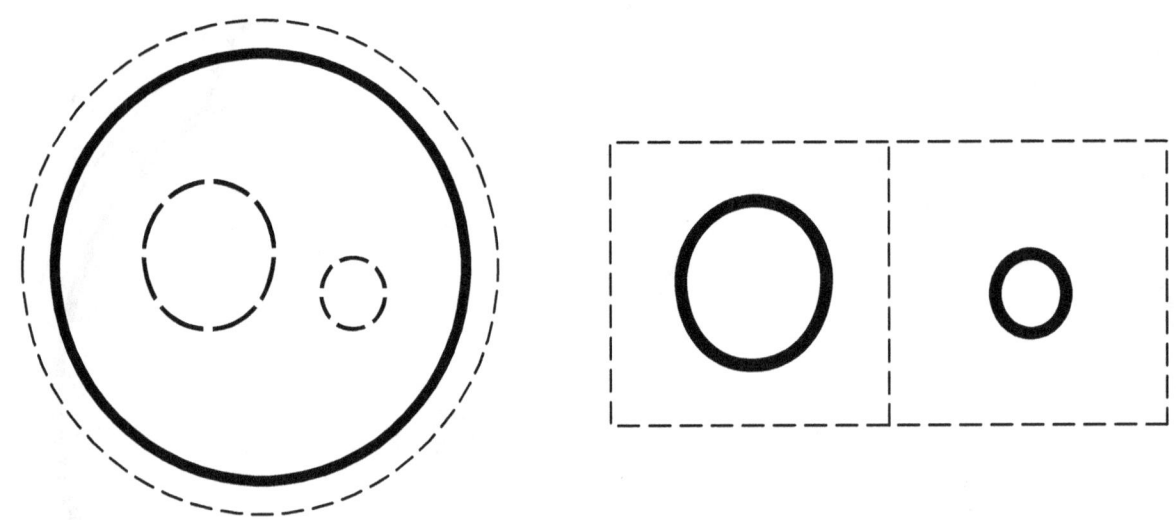

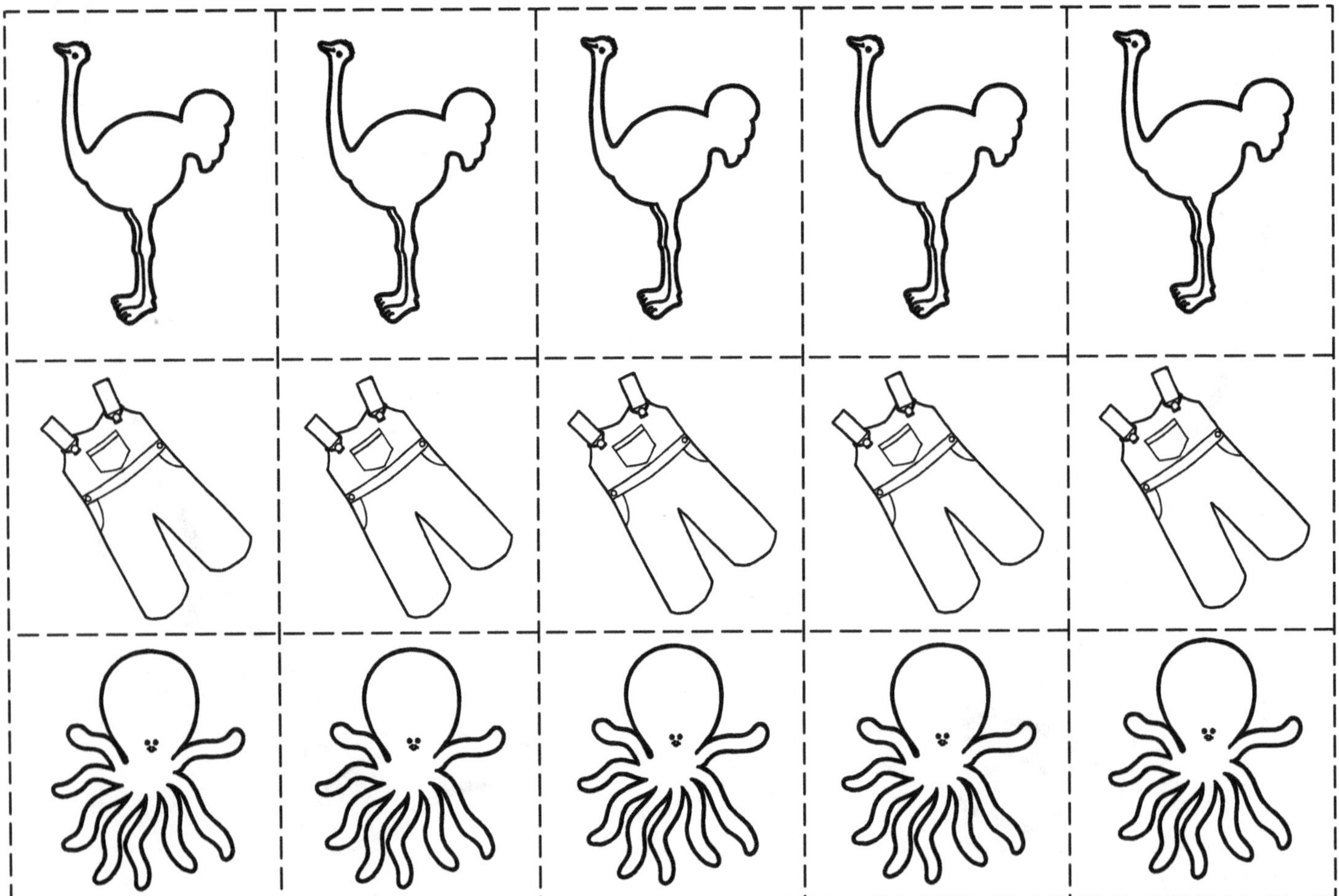

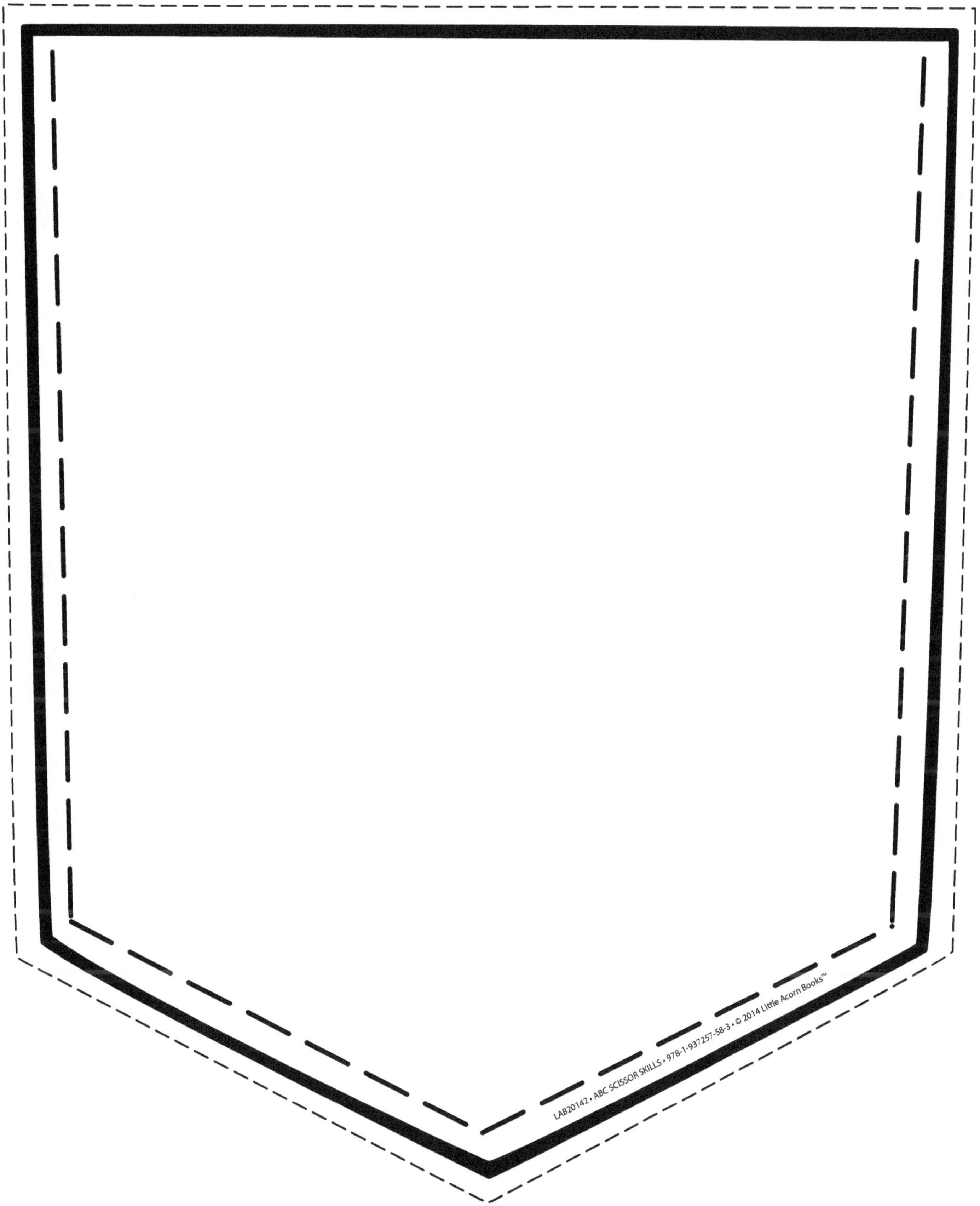
LAB20142 • ABC SCISSOR SKILLS • 978-1-937257-58-3 • © 2014 Little Acorn Books™

Letter Pp and Pictures

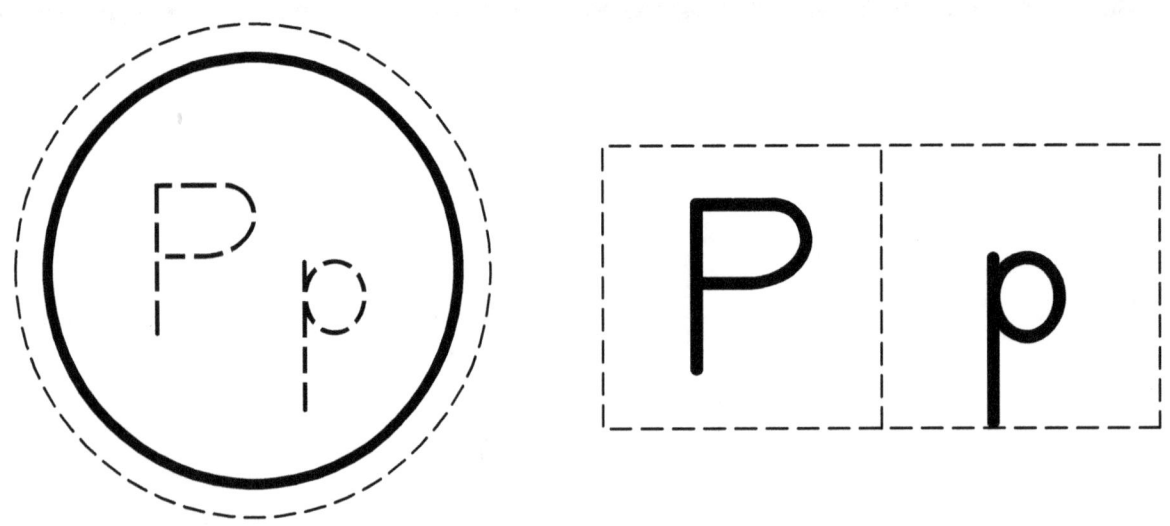

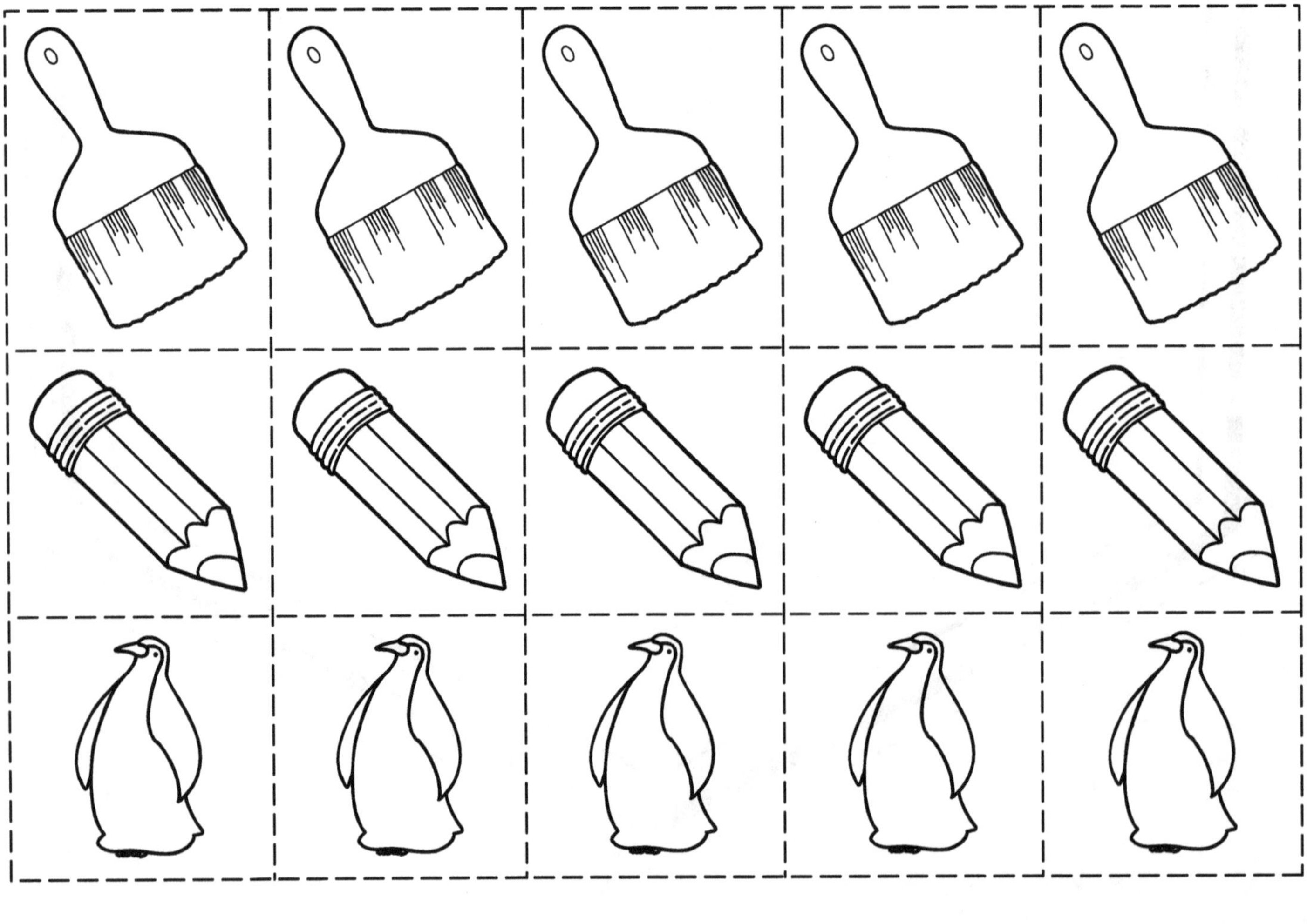

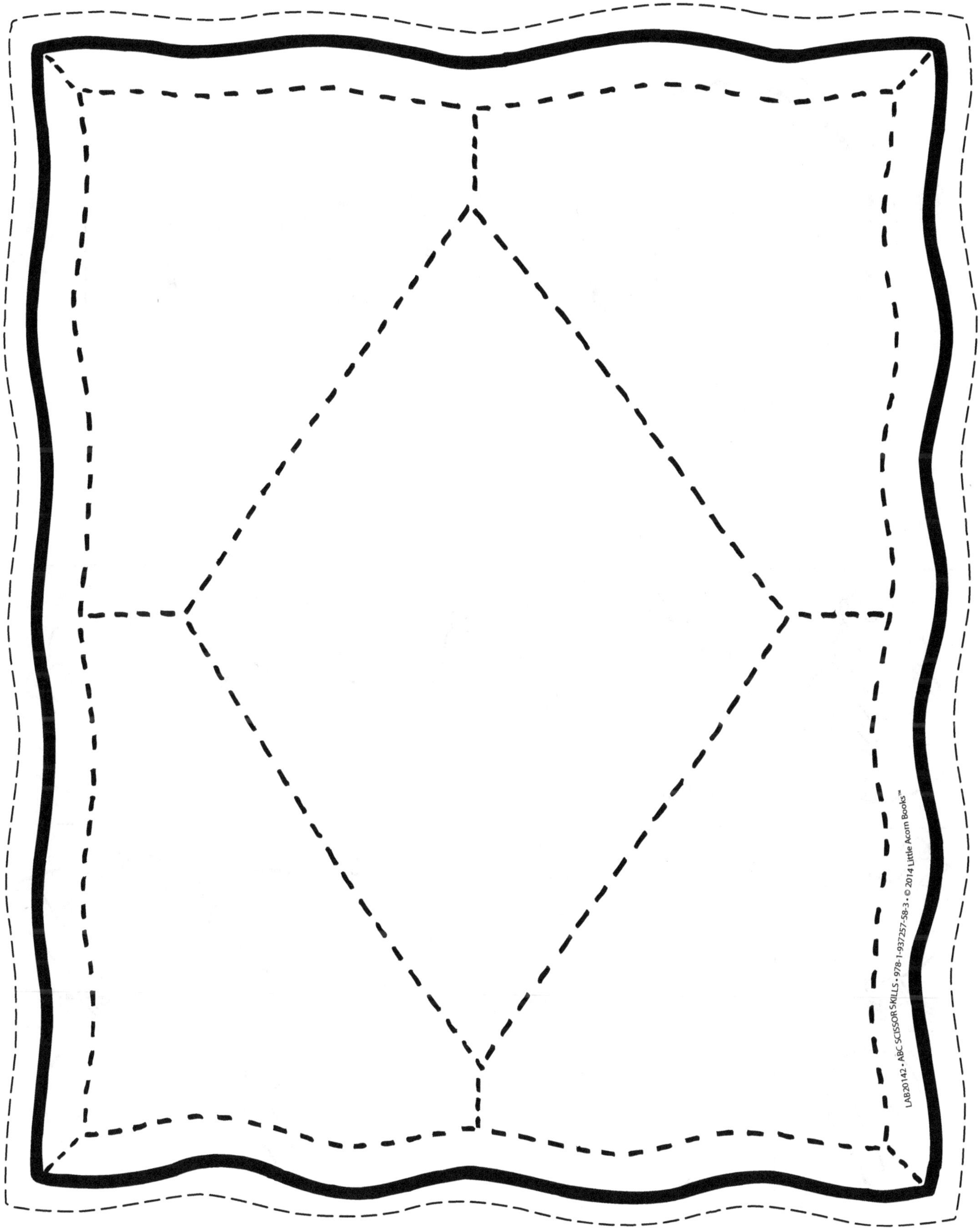
LAB20142 • ABC SCISSOR SKILLS • 978-1-937257-58-3 • © 2014 Little Acorn Books™

Letter Qq and Pictures

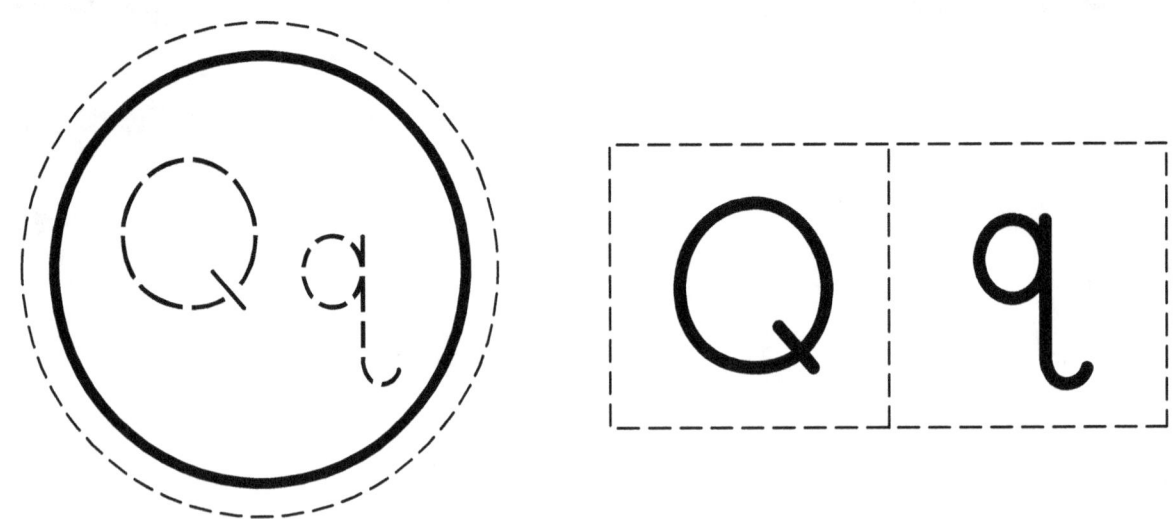

Rabbit

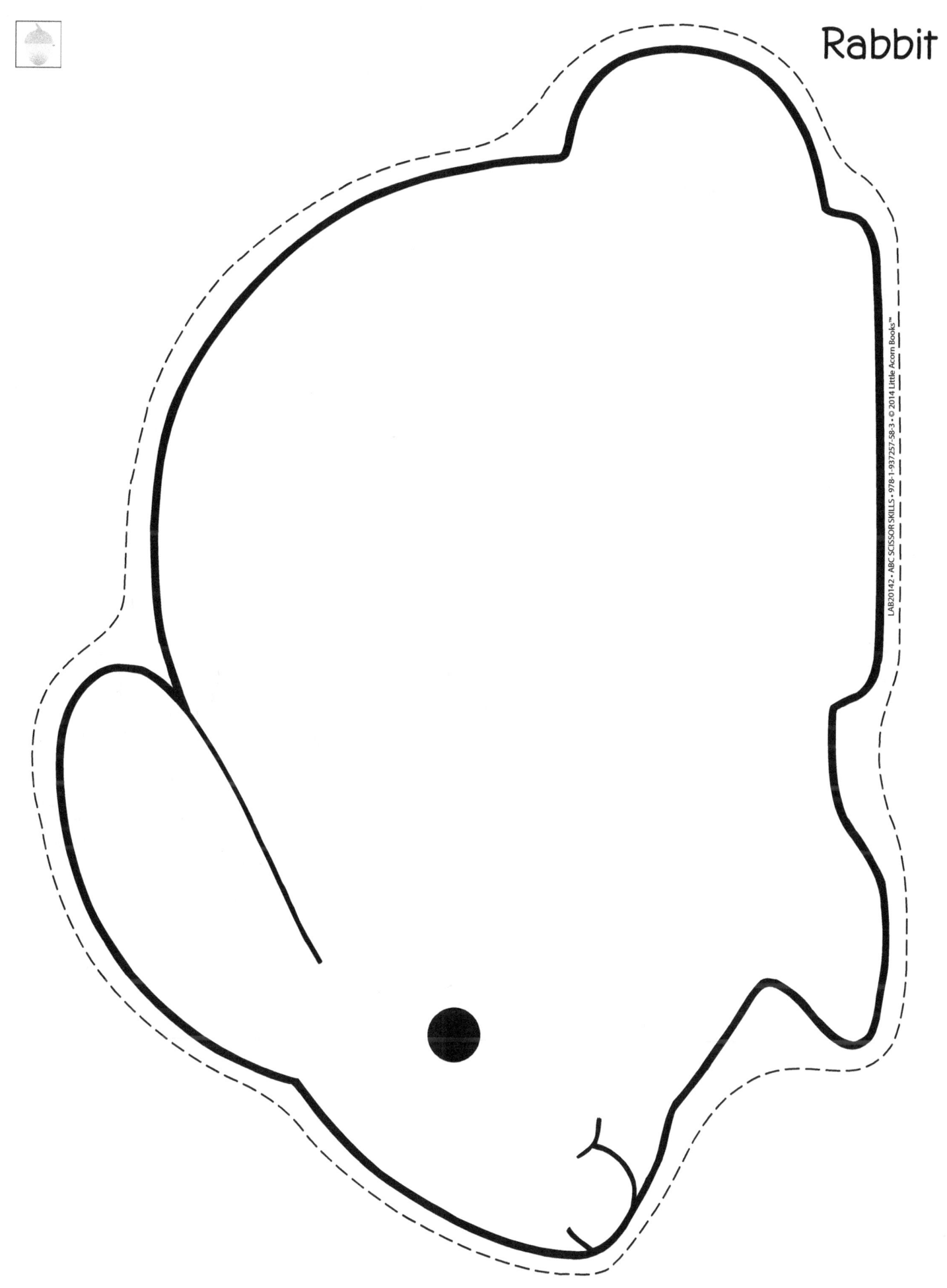

Letter Rr and Pictures

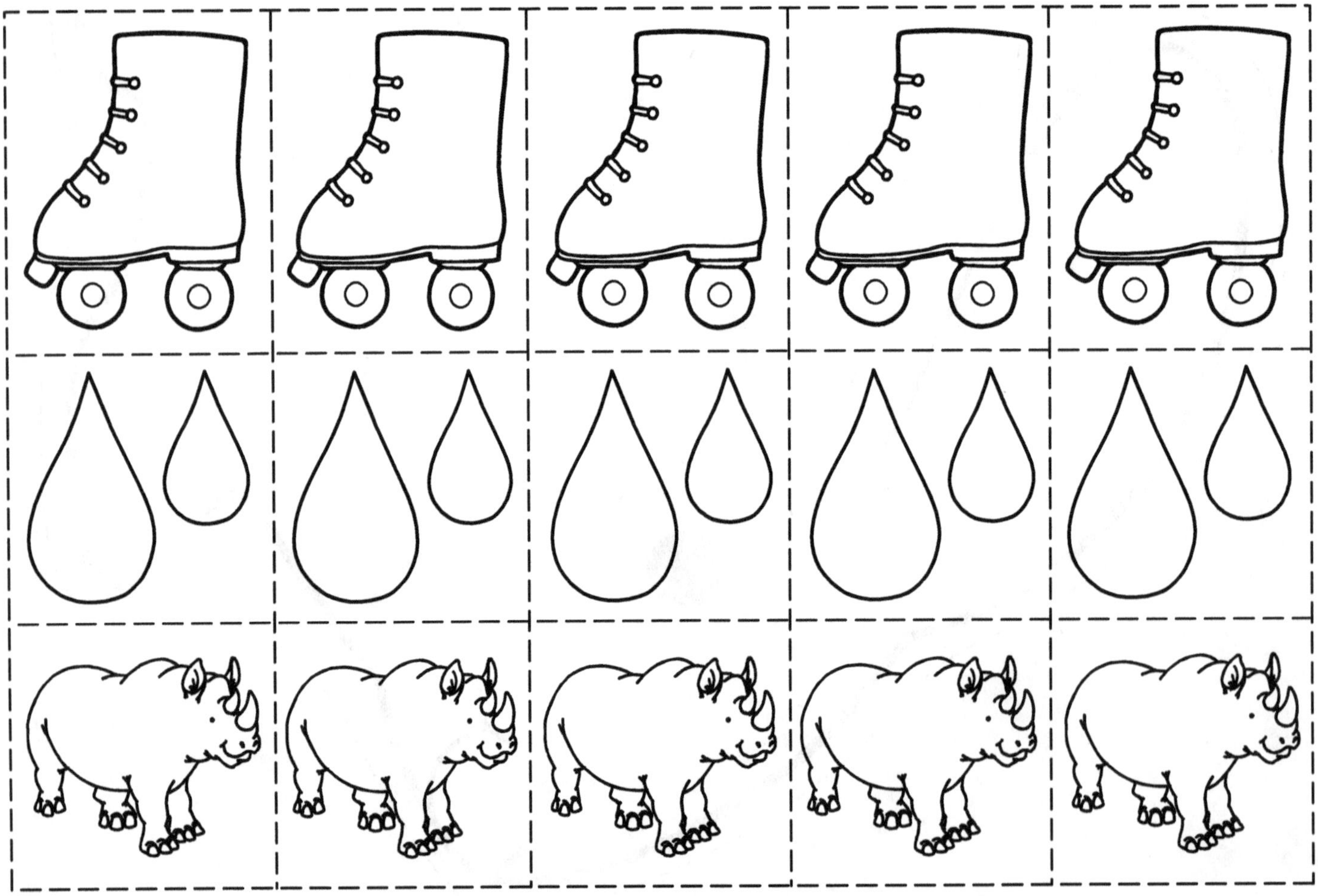

44

Snowman

Letter Ss and Pictures

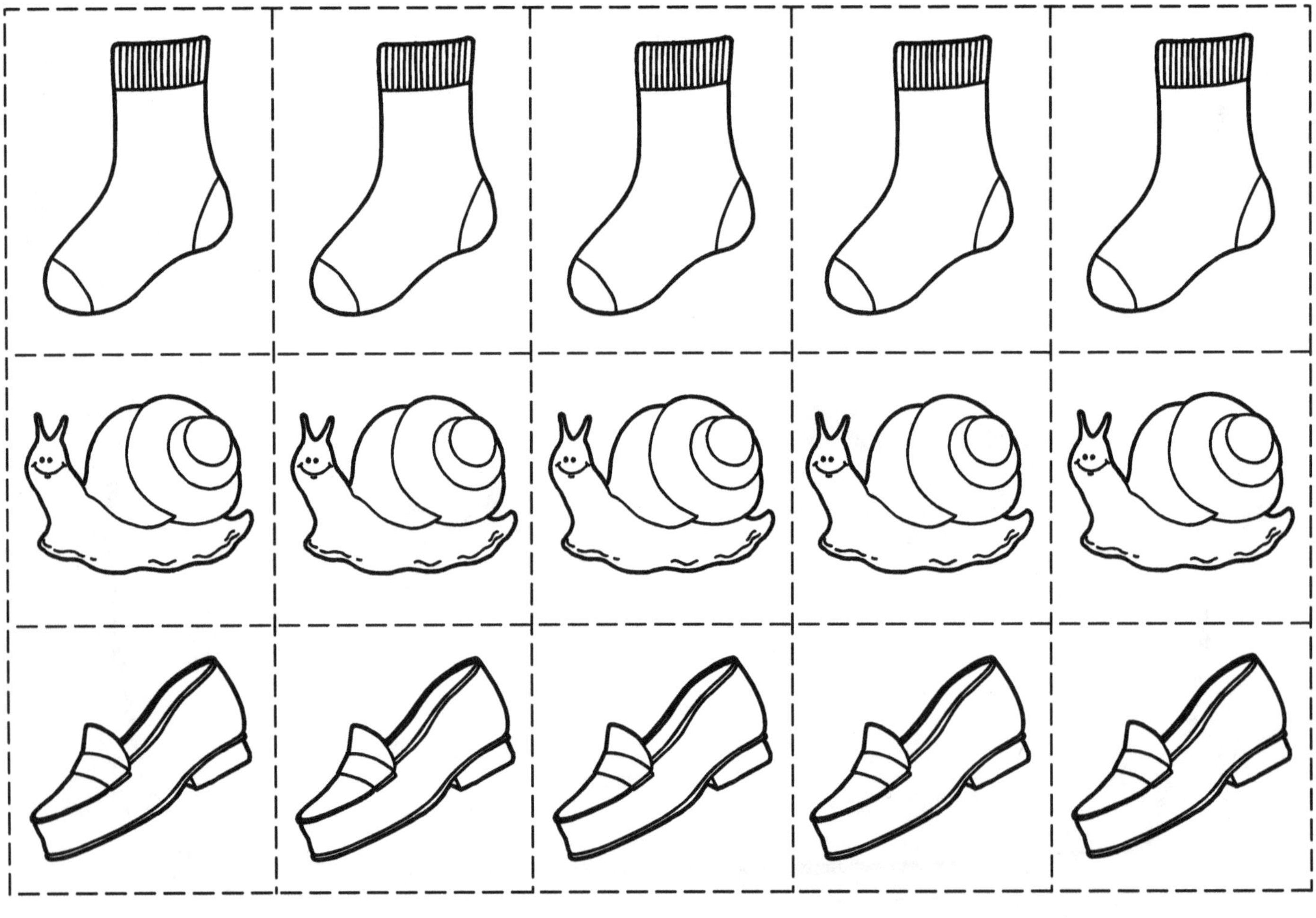

Tree

Letter Tt and Pictures

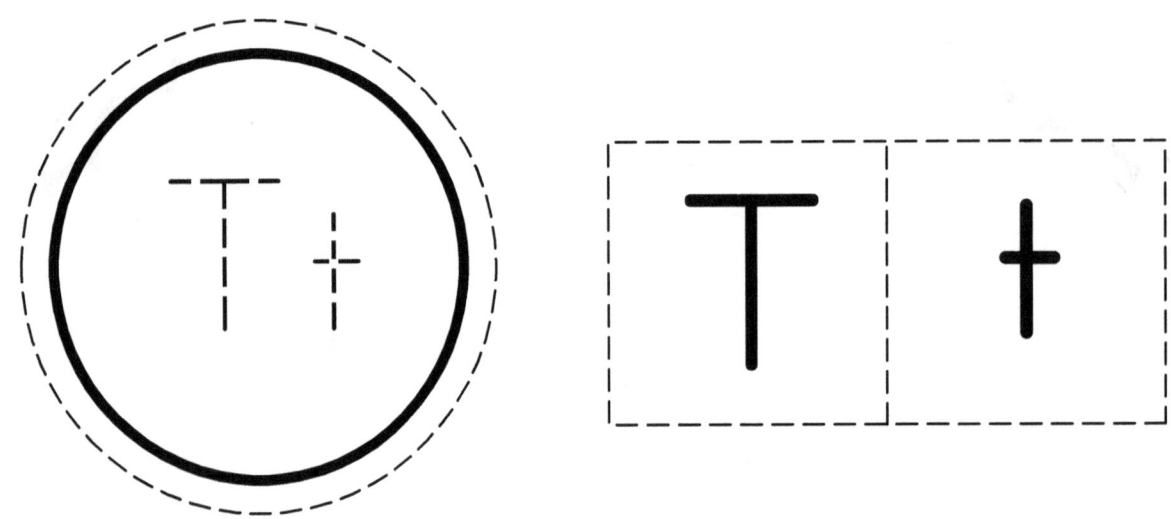

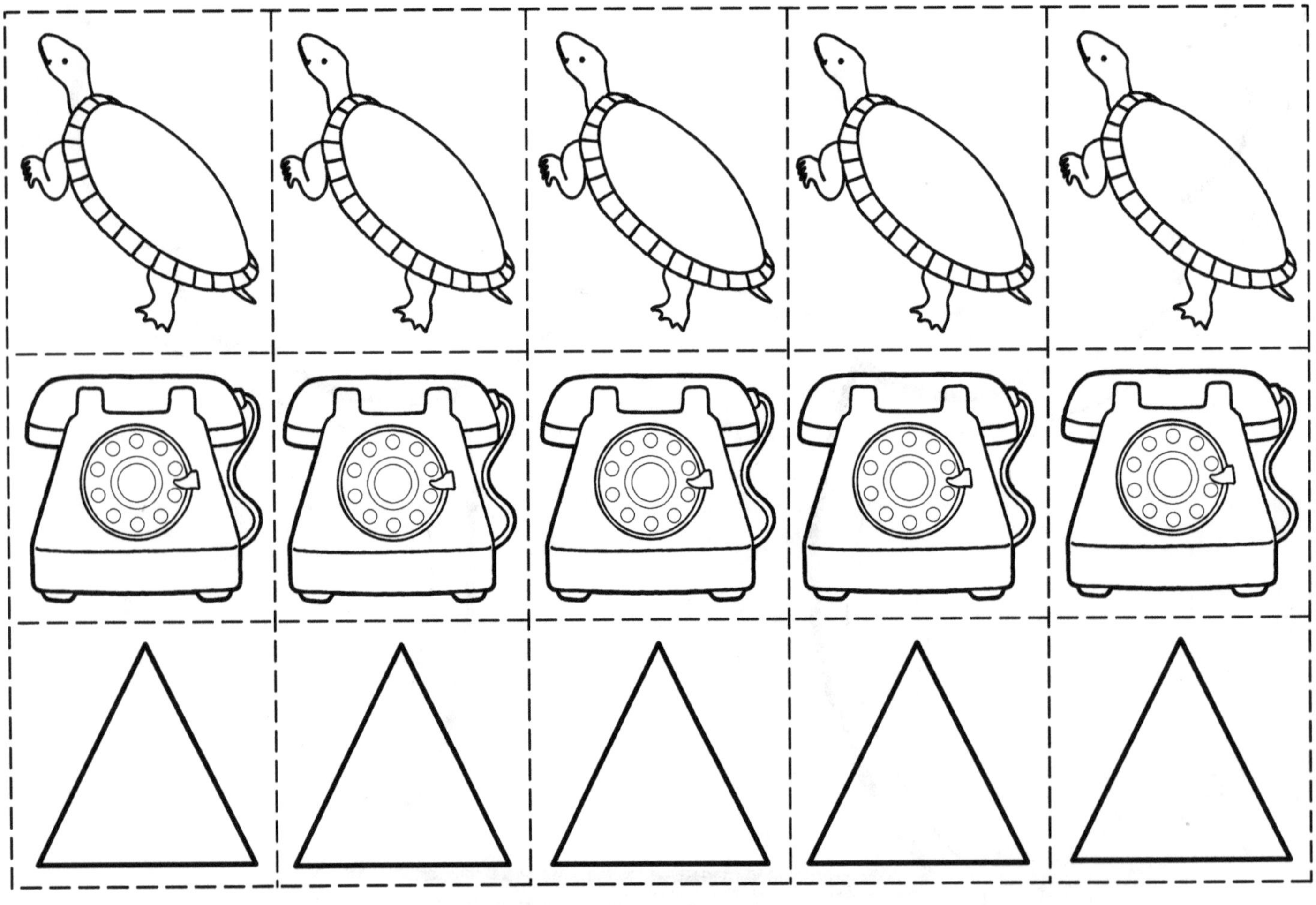

Umbrella

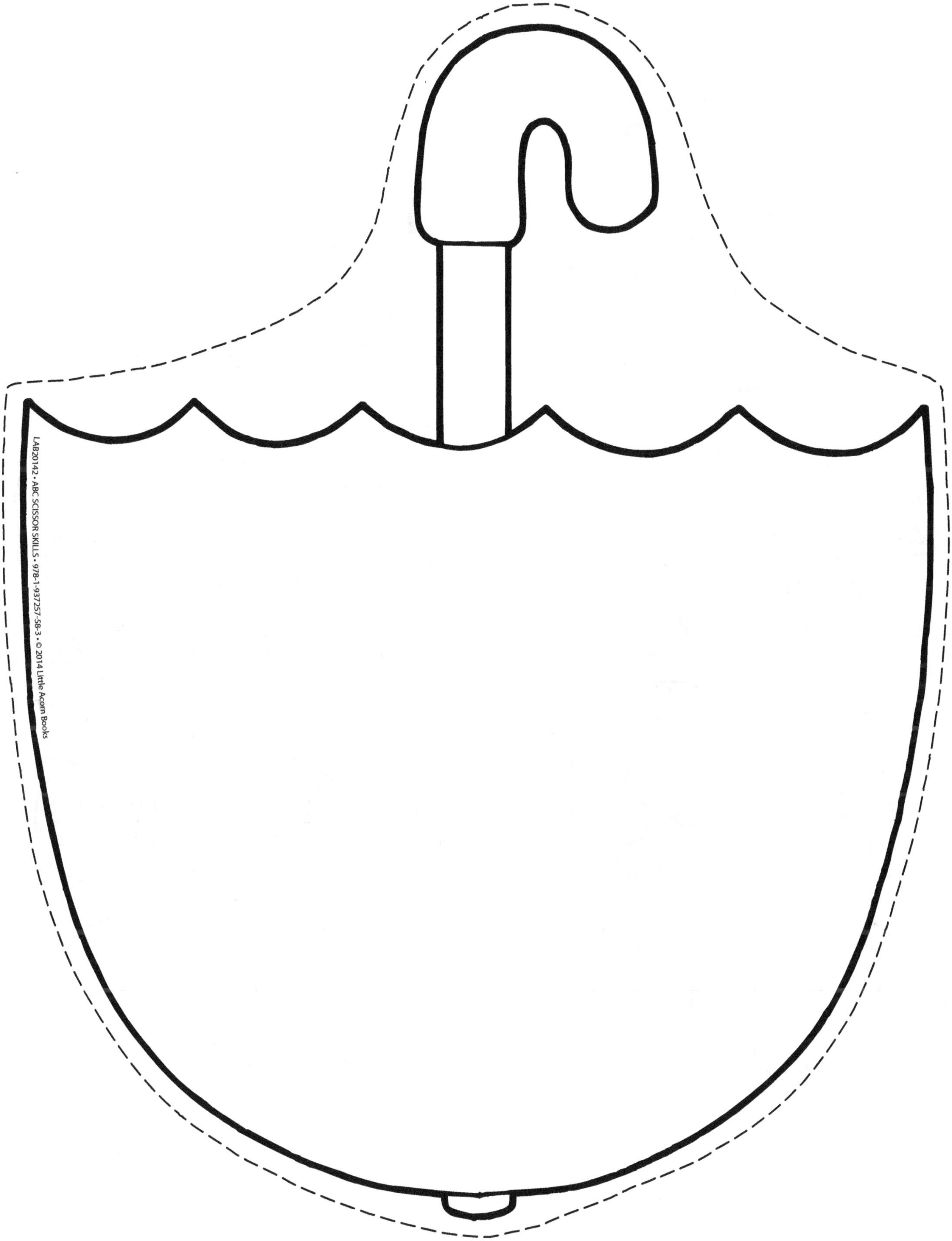

Letter Uu and Pictures

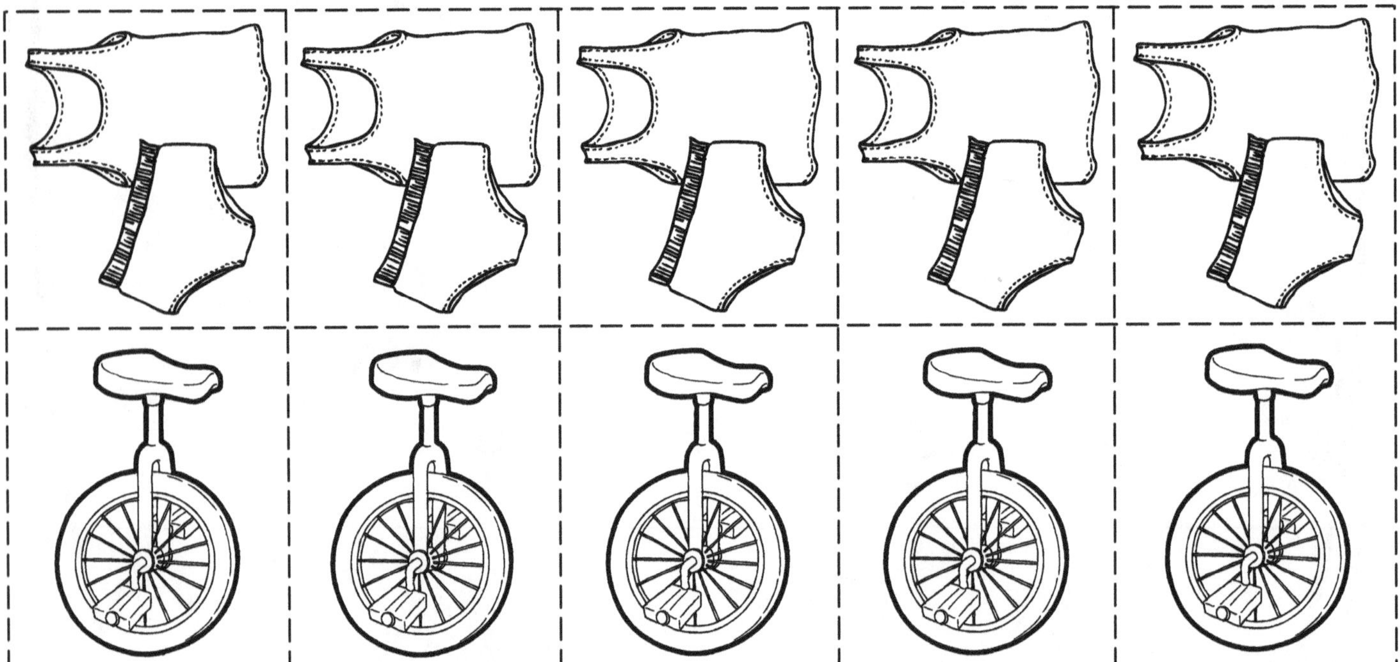

Vest

Letter Vv and Pictures

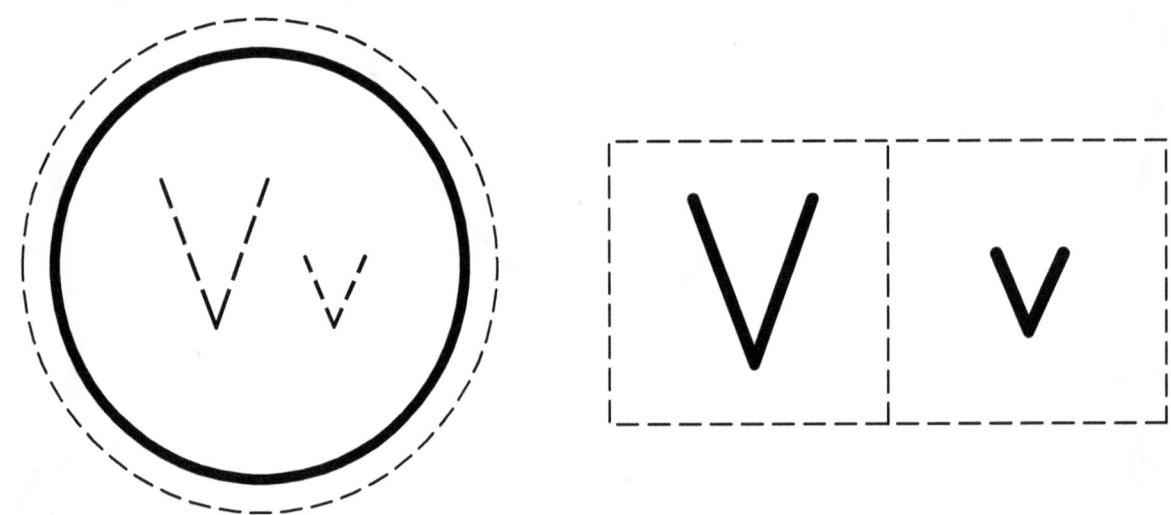

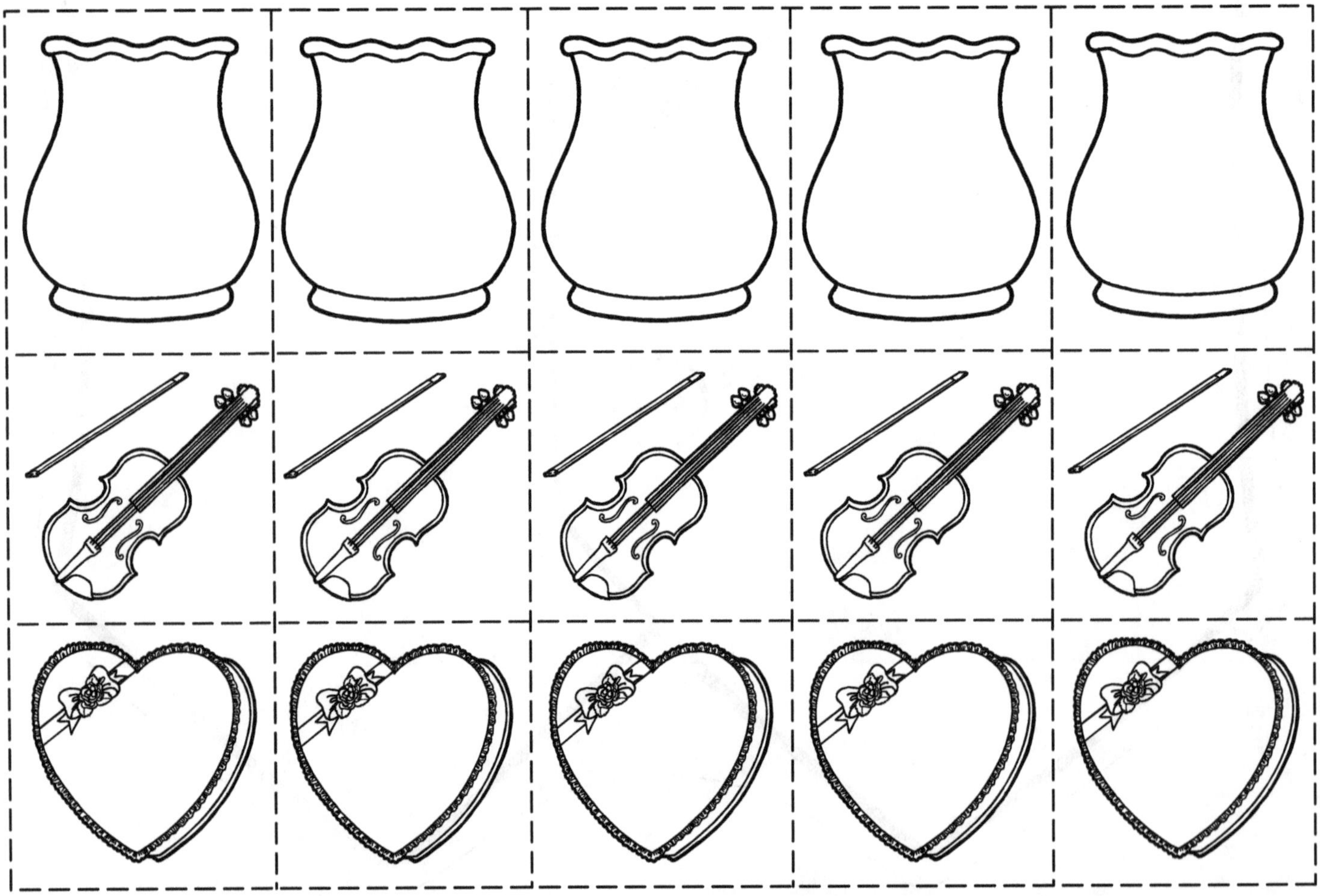

Whale

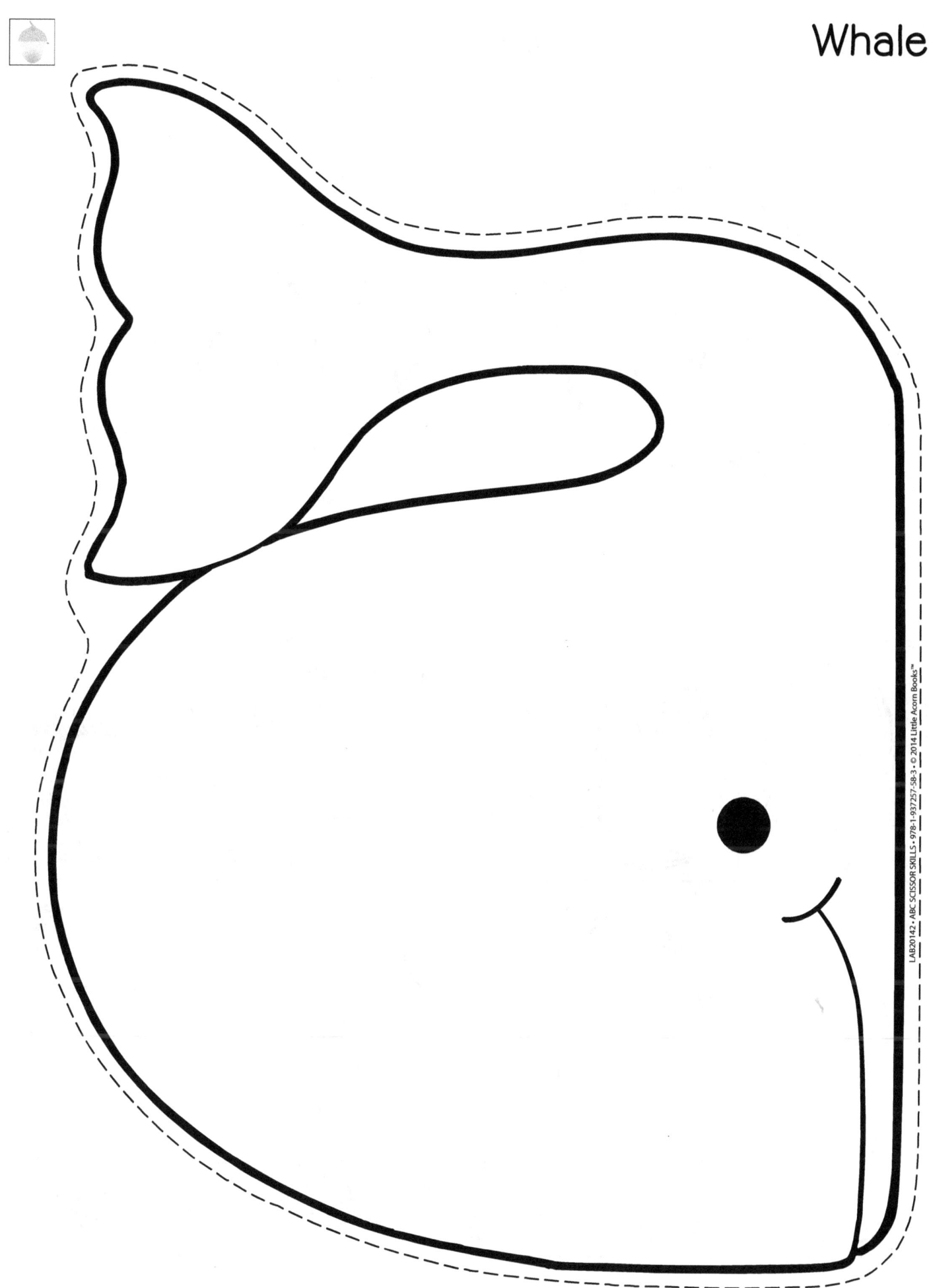

Letter Ww and Pictures

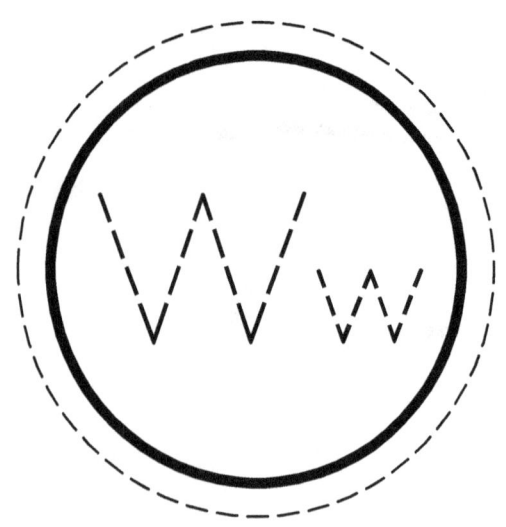
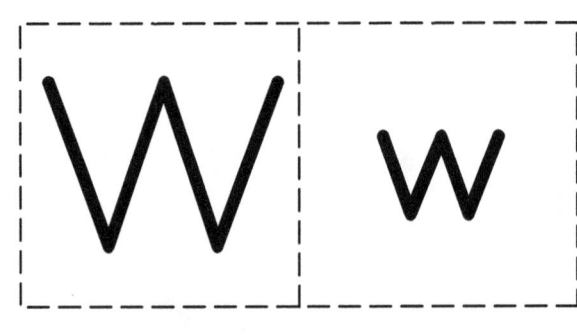

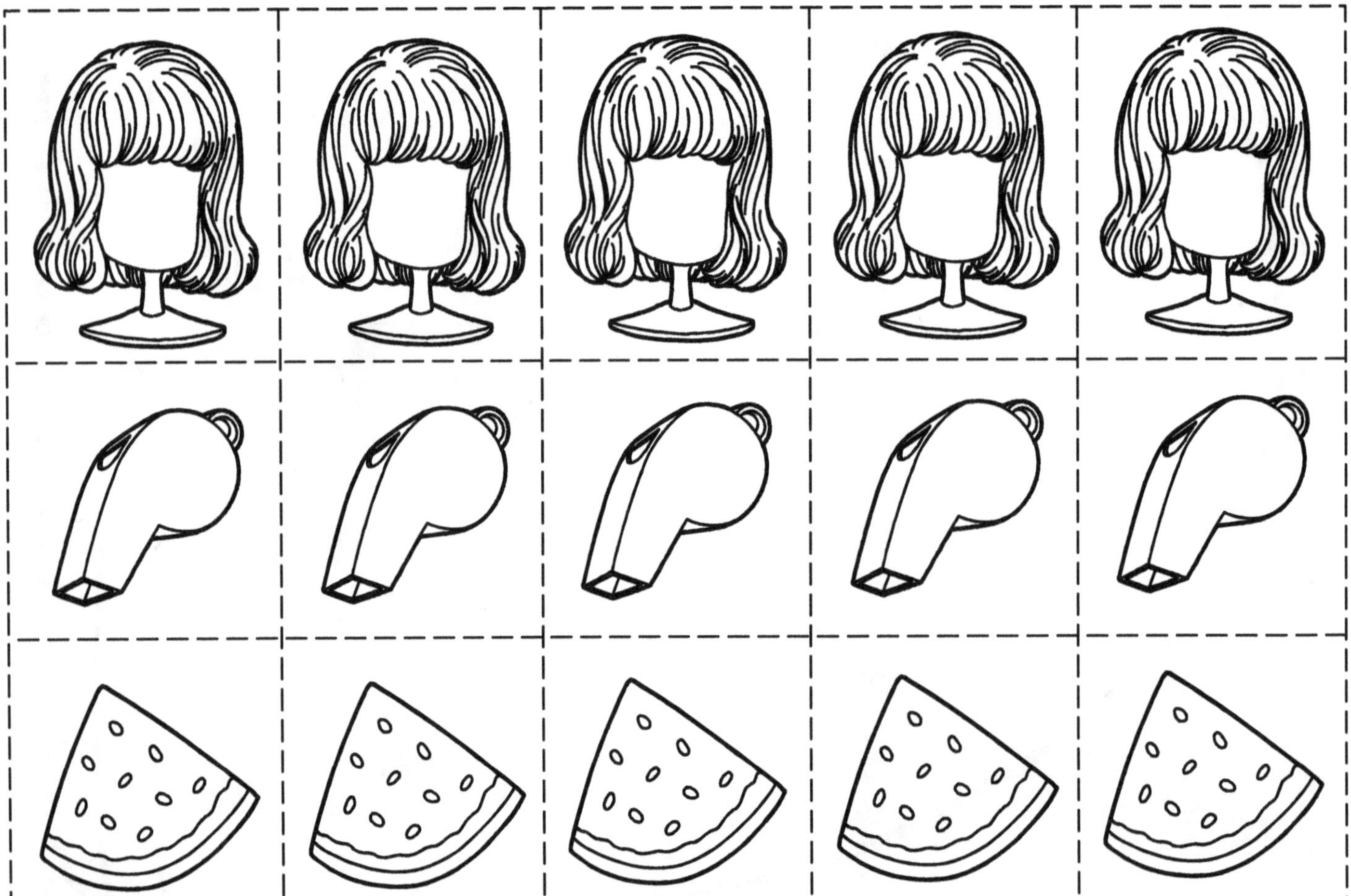

A Giant X

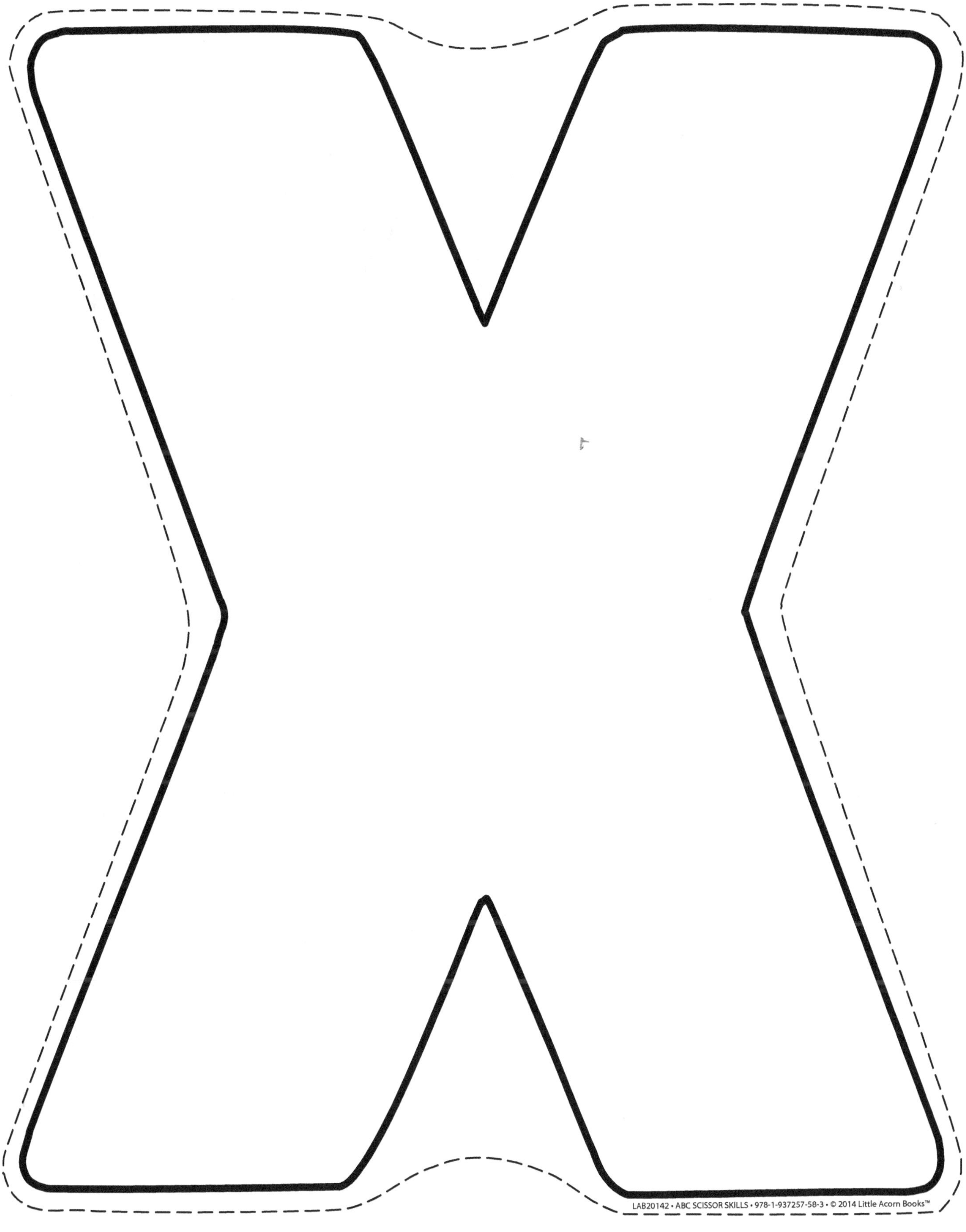
LAB20142 • ABC SCISSOR SKILLS • 978-1-937257-58-3 • © 2014 Little Acorn Books™

Letter Xx and Pictures

X x

X x

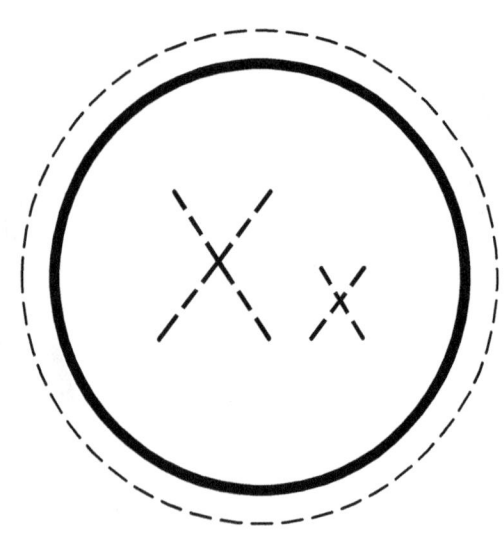

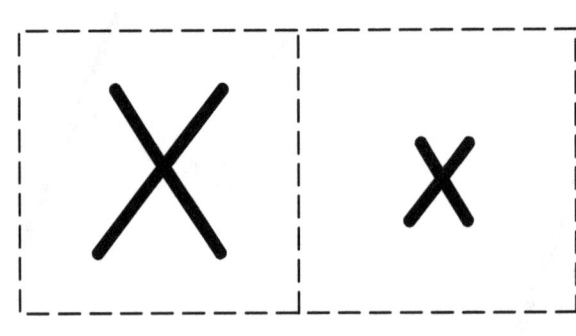

xantusia
xantusia
xantusia
xantusia
xantusia

LAB20142P • ABC SCISSOR SKILLS • 978-1-937257-58-3 •

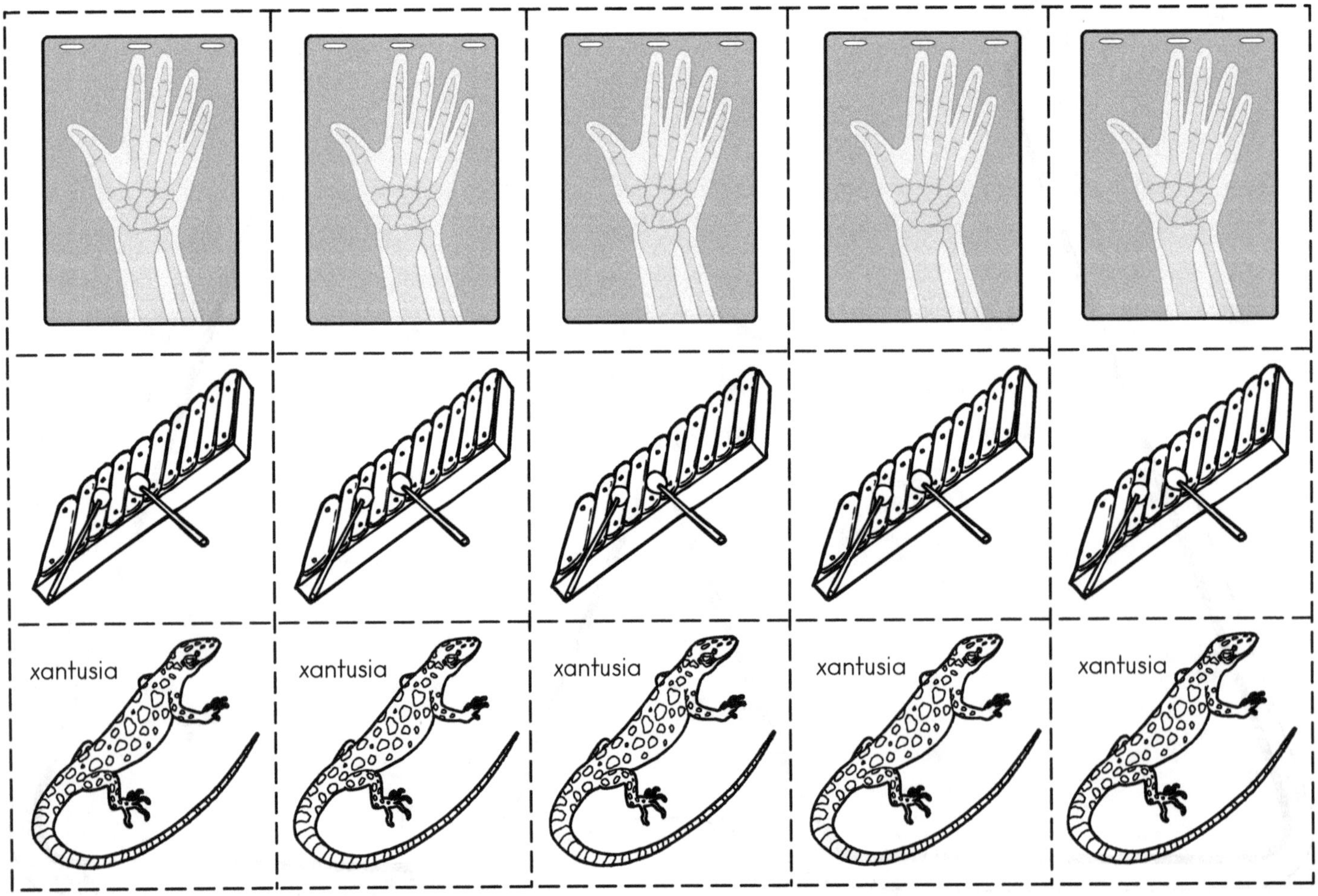

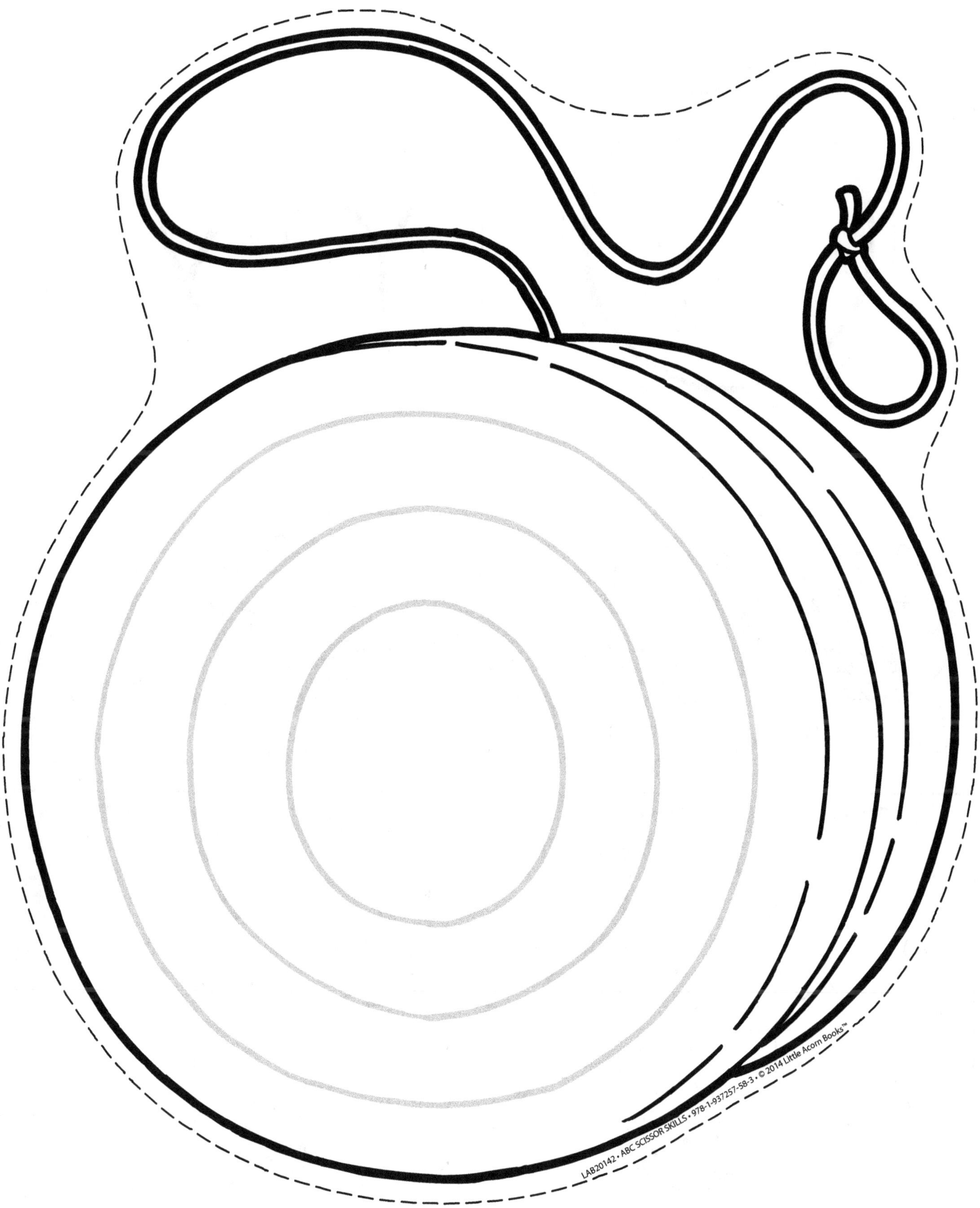
LAB20142 • ABC SCISSOR SKILLS • 978-1-937257-58-3 • © 2014 Little Acorn Books™

Letter Yy and Pictures

Y y

yawn
yawn
yawn
yawn
yawn

LAB20142P • ABC SCISSOR SKILLS • 978-1-937257-58-3 •

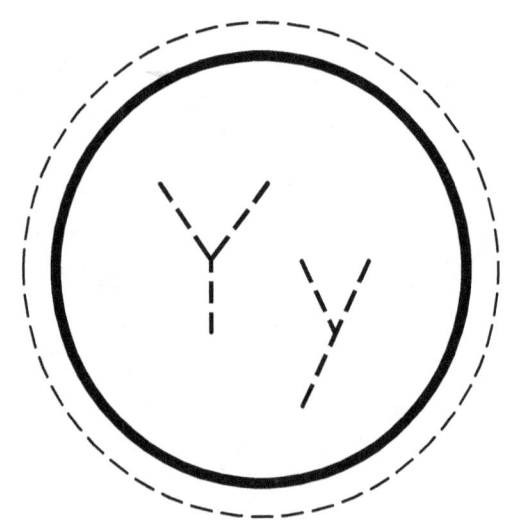

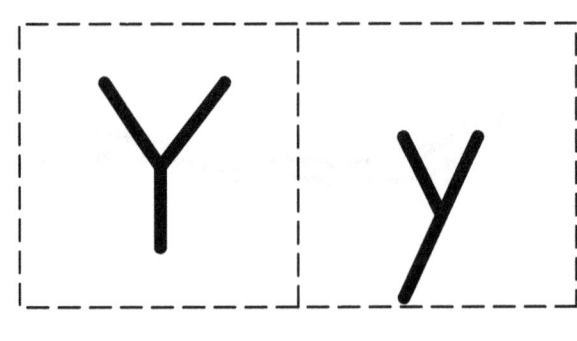

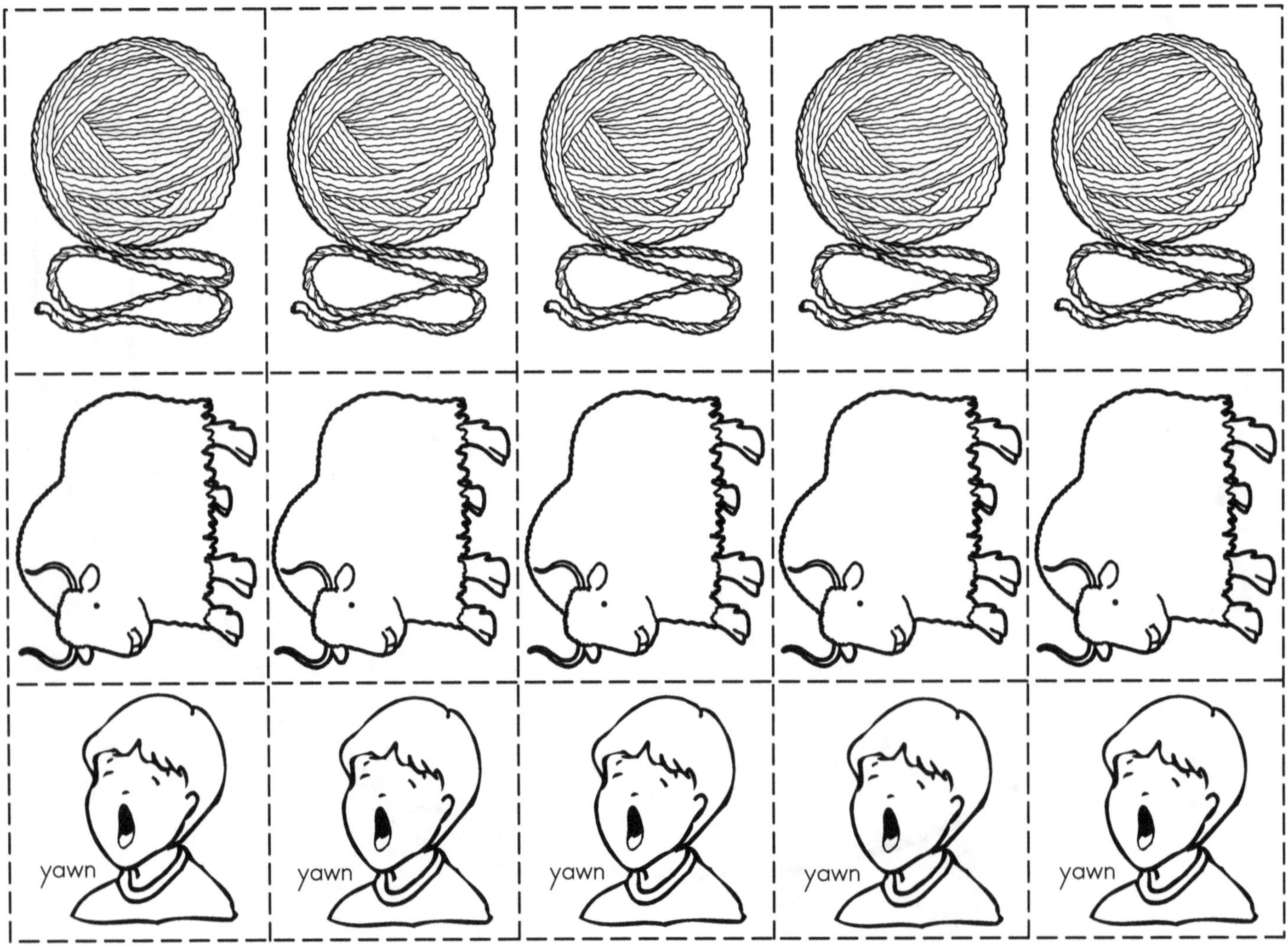

Zebra

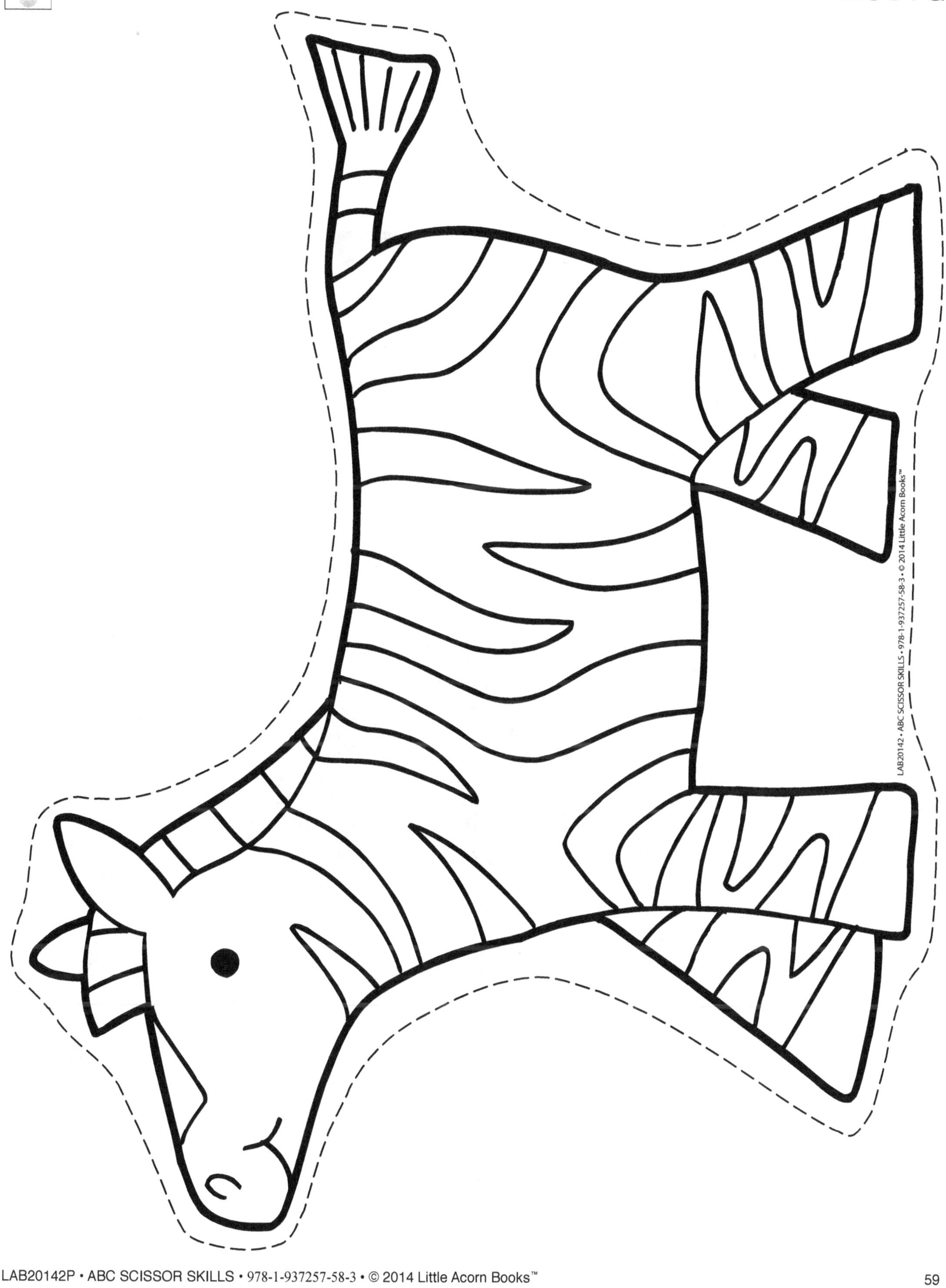

Letter Zz and Pictures

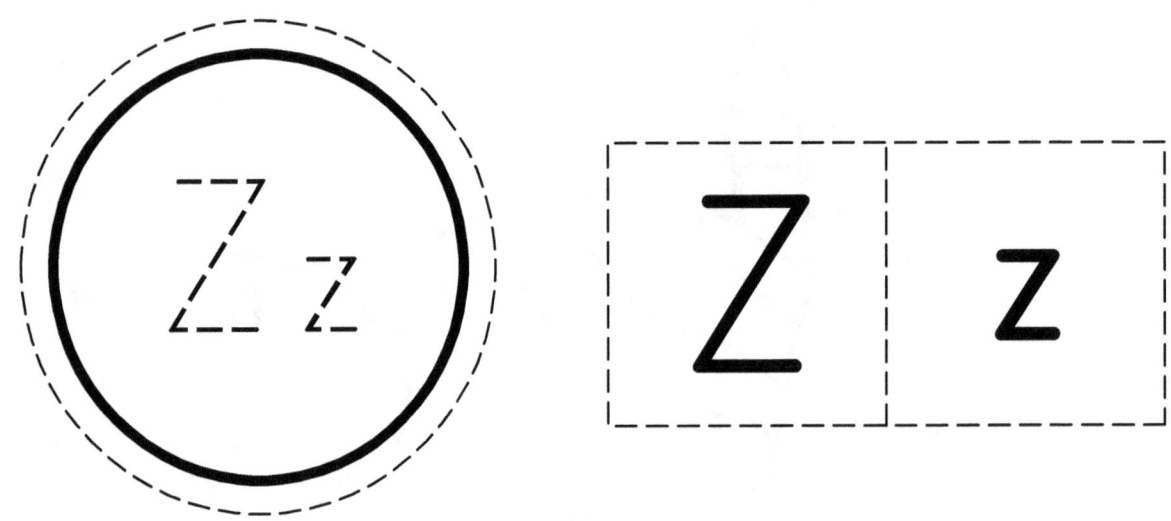

zipper	zipper	zipper	zipper	zipper
zither	zither	zither	zither	zither
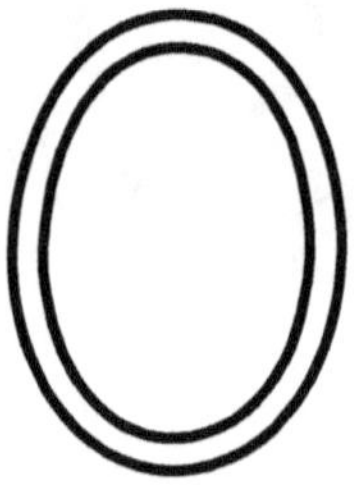 zero	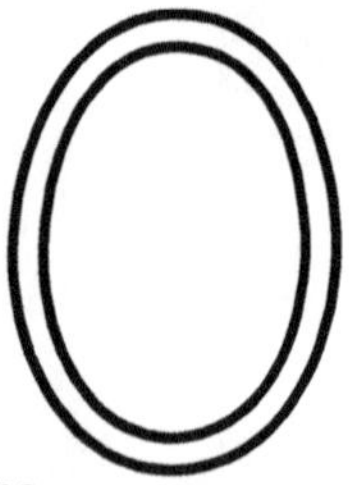 zero	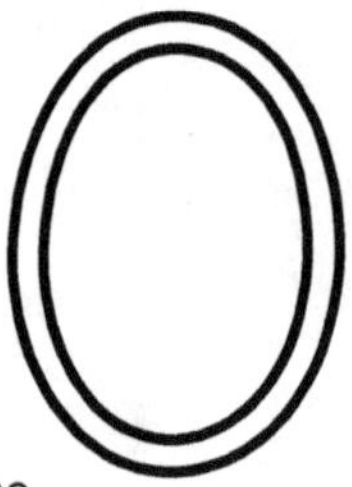 zero	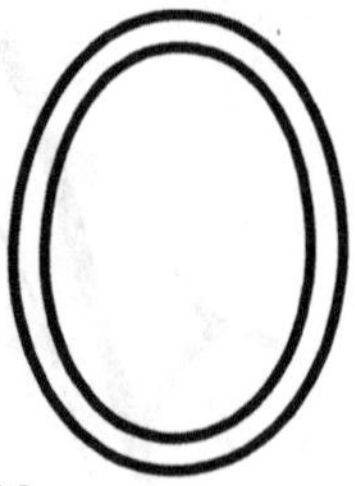 zero	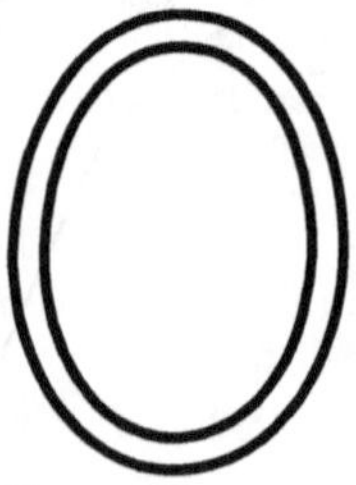 zero

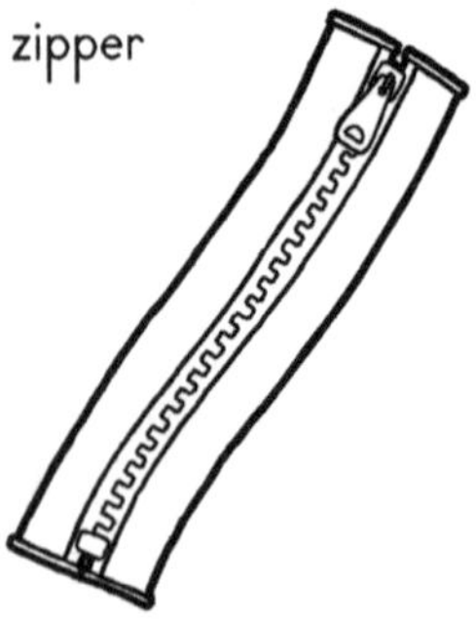

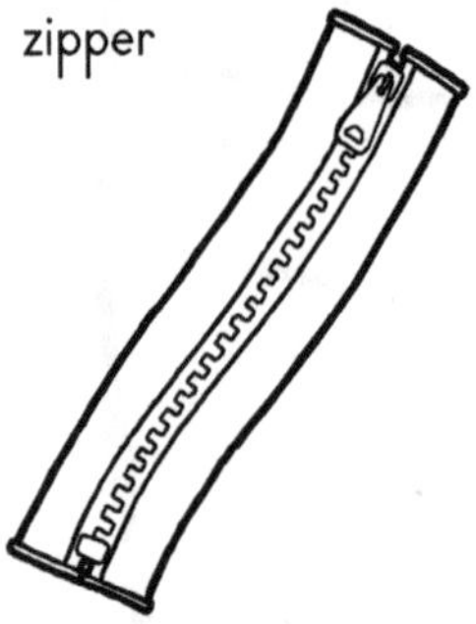

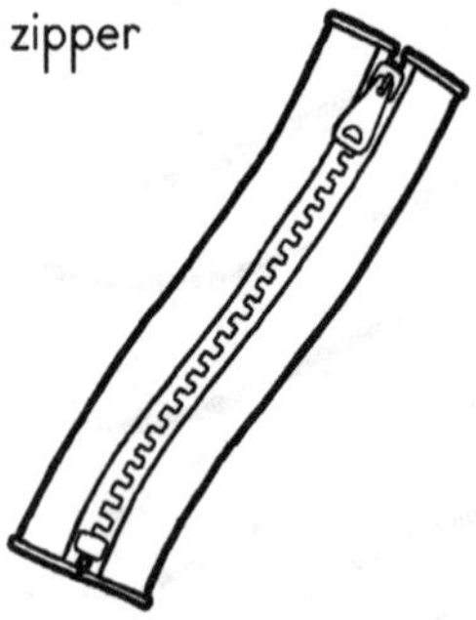

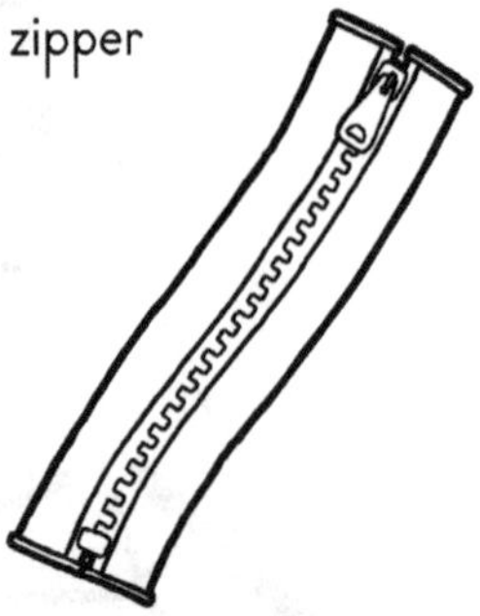

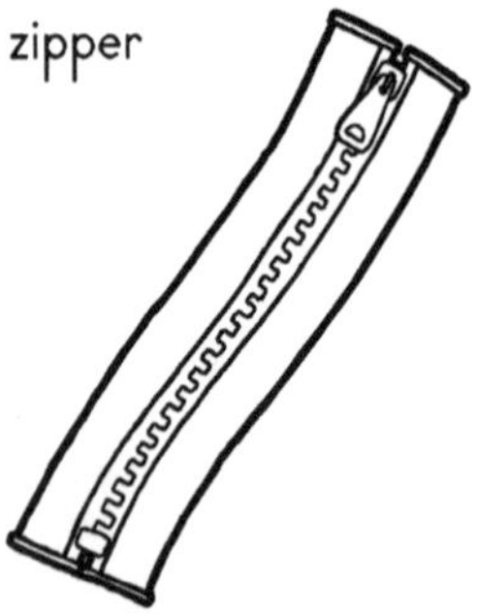

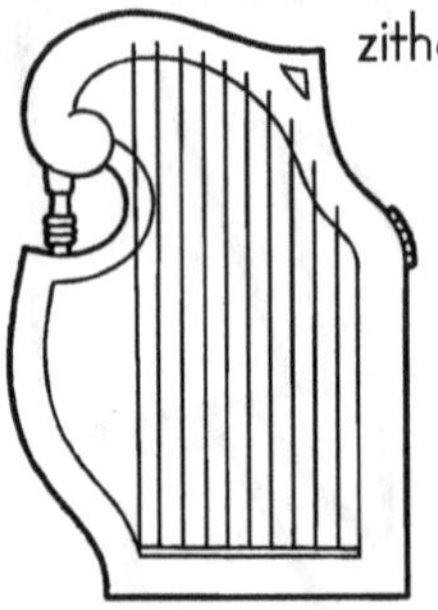

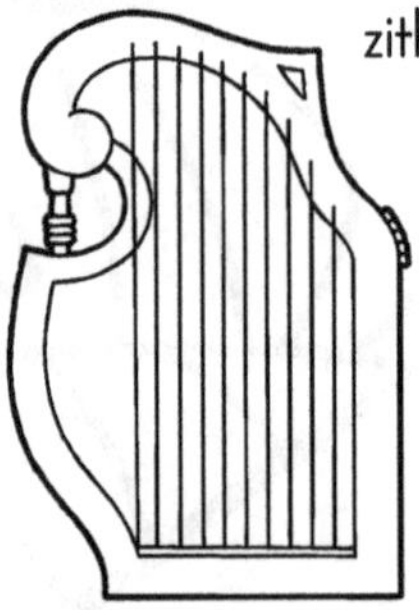

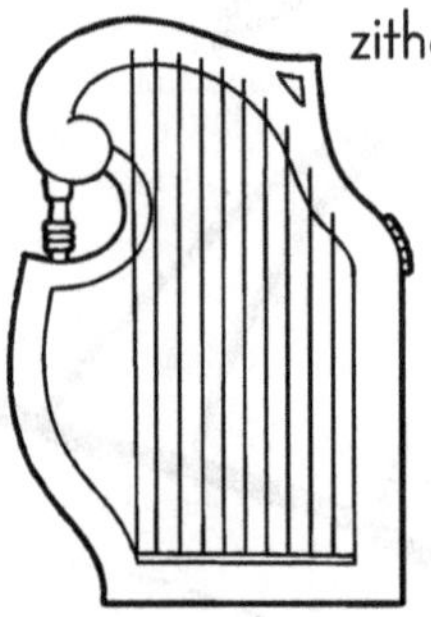

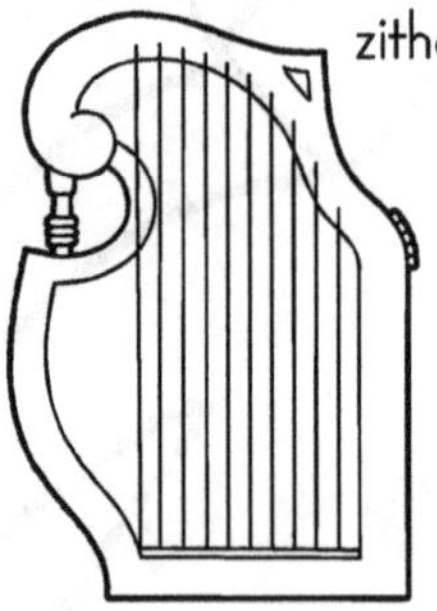

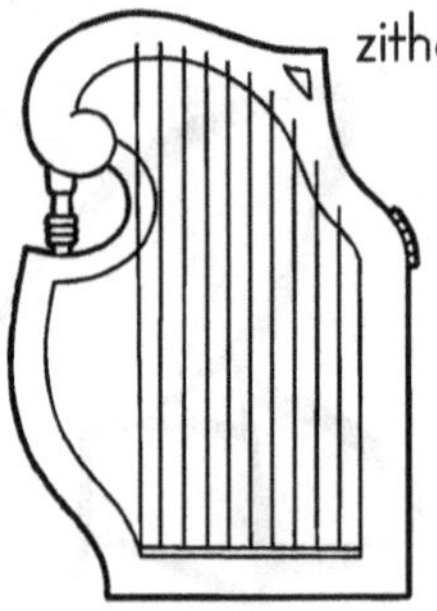

More Alphabet Pictures

A

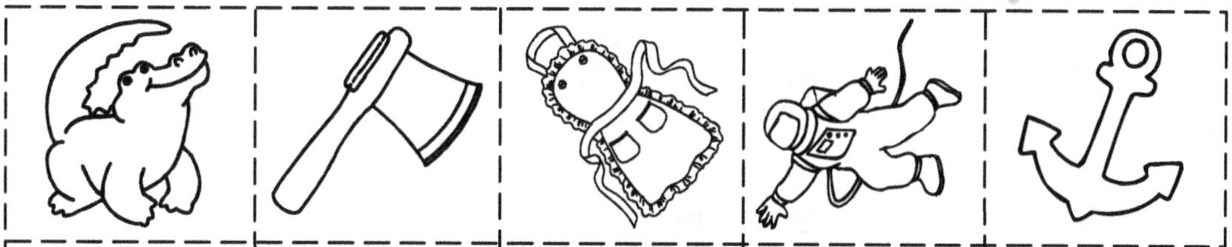

B

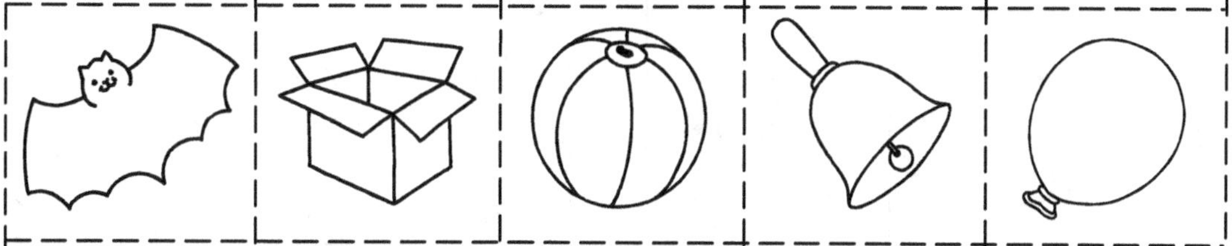

C

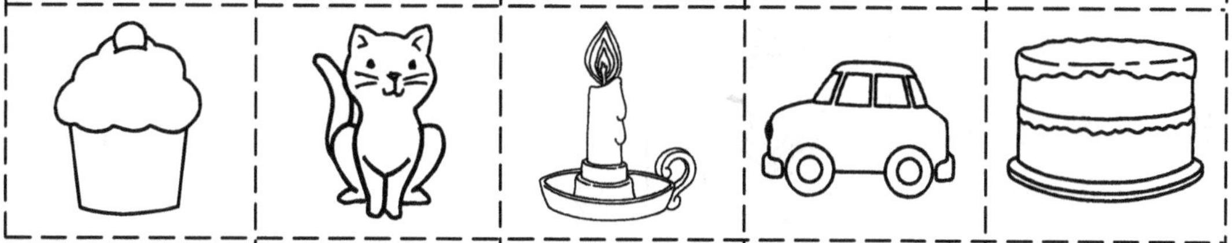

D

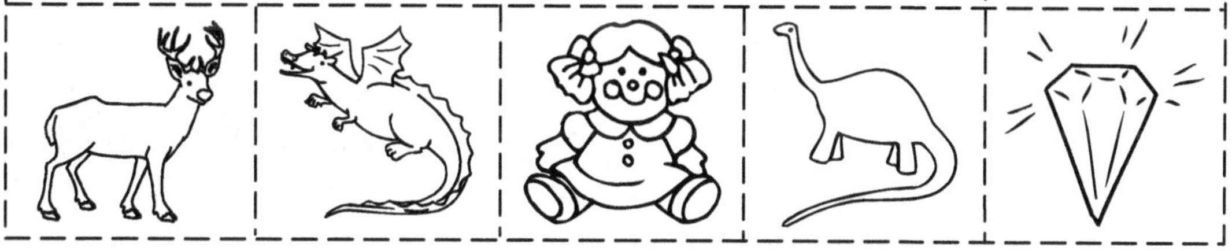

E

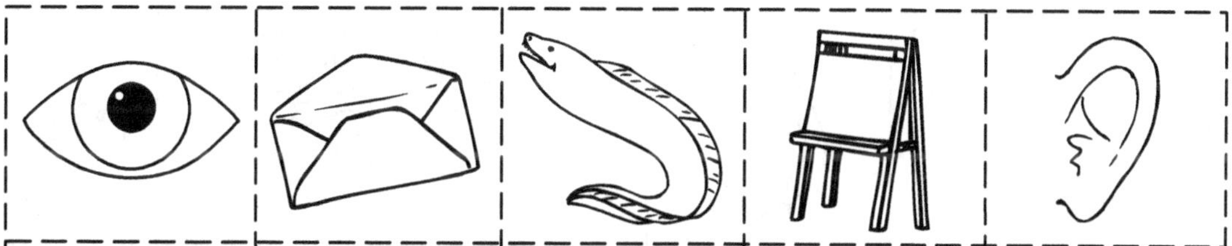

F

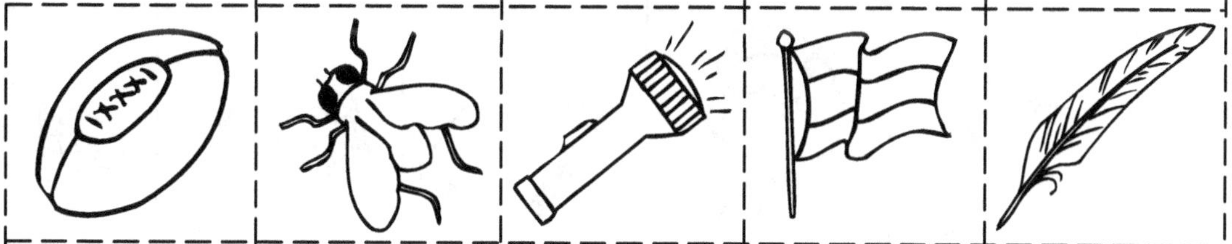

G

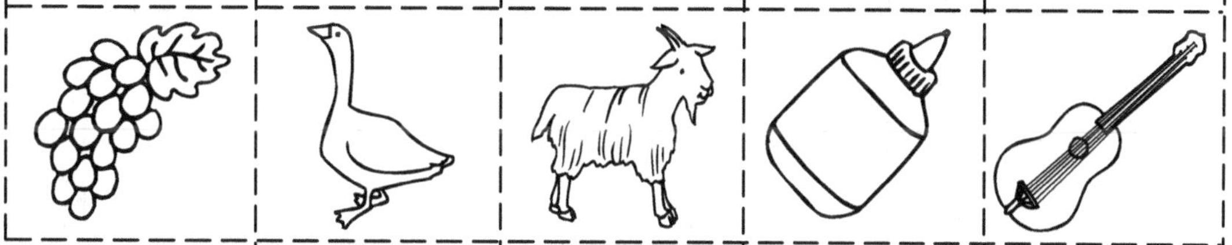

H

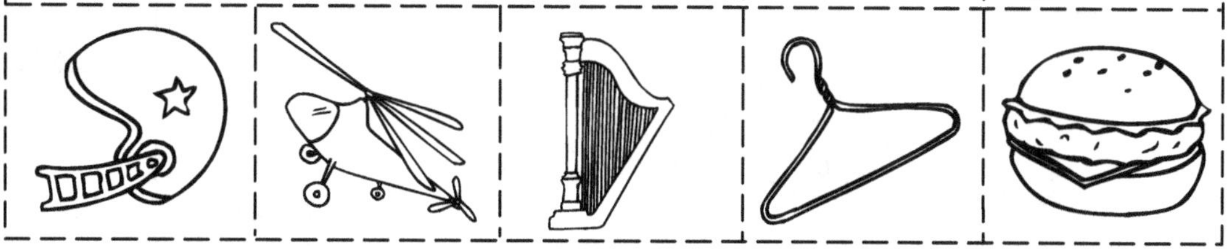

More Alphabet Pictures

I

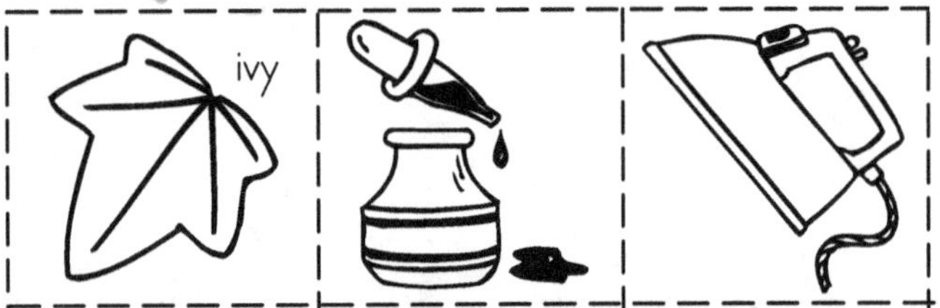

J

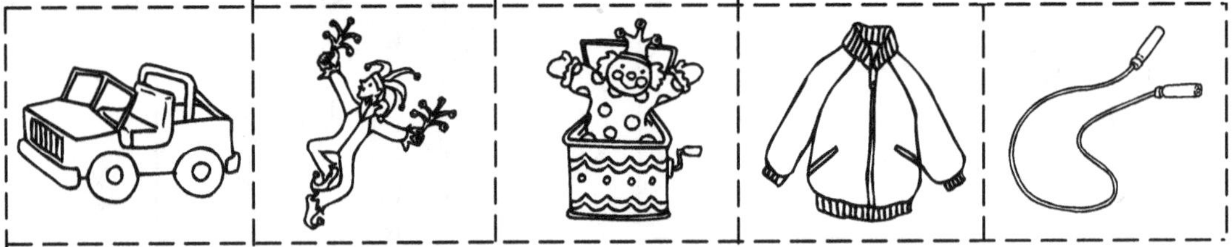

K

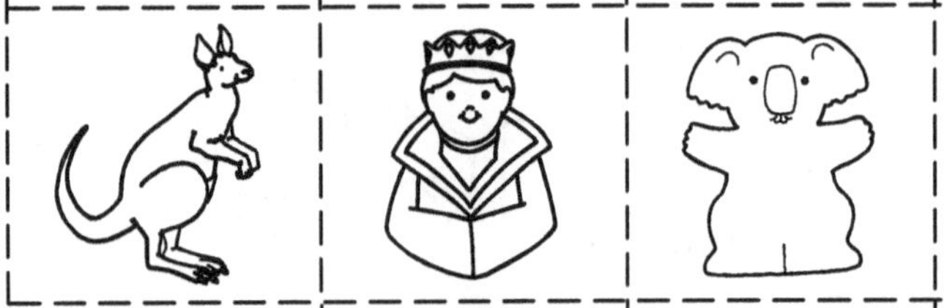

L

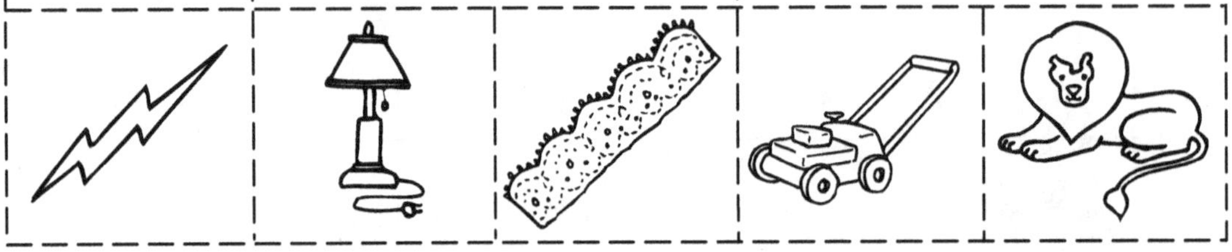

M

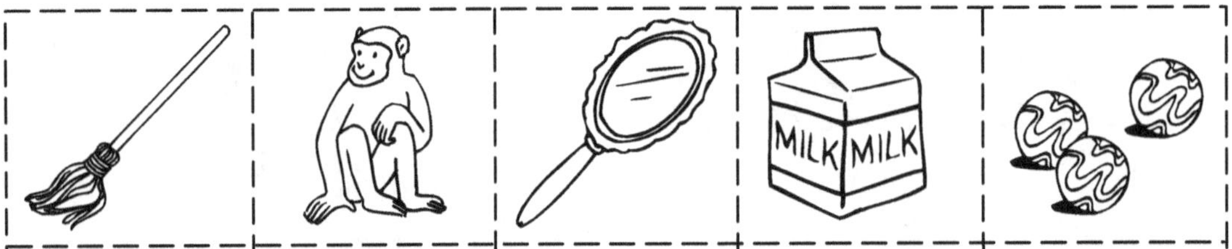

N

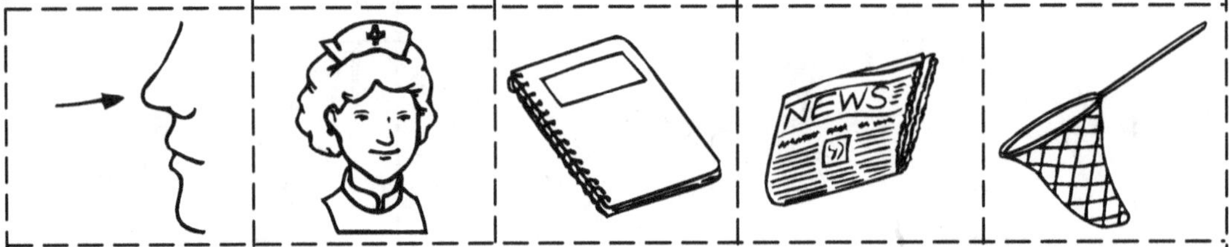

O

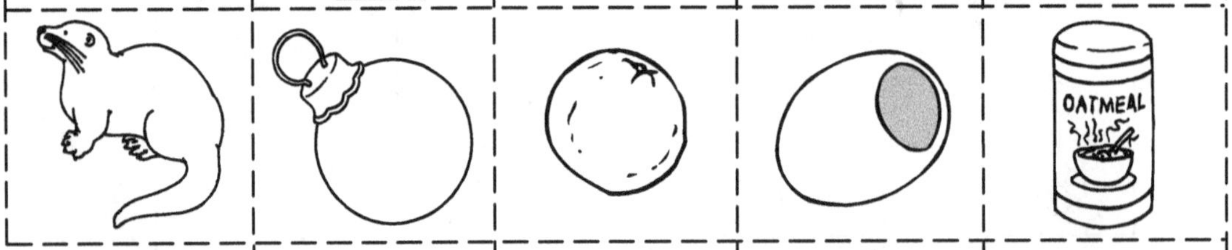

P

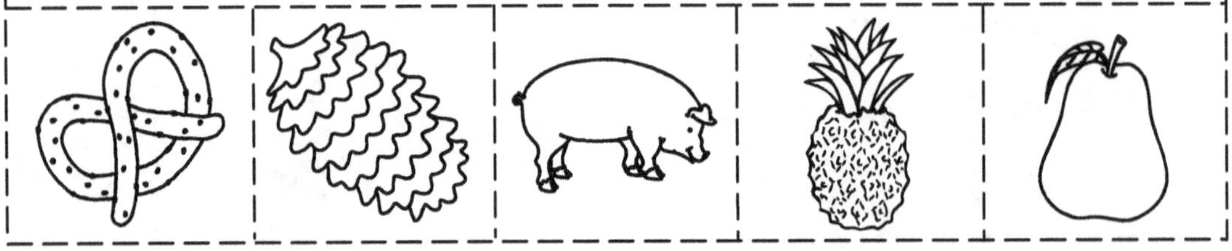

More Alphabet Pictures

Q	quetzal		Shhh!		
R					
S					
T					
U					
V		vole	visor	vicuña	
W					
Y Z		zebu		zeppelin	zigzag

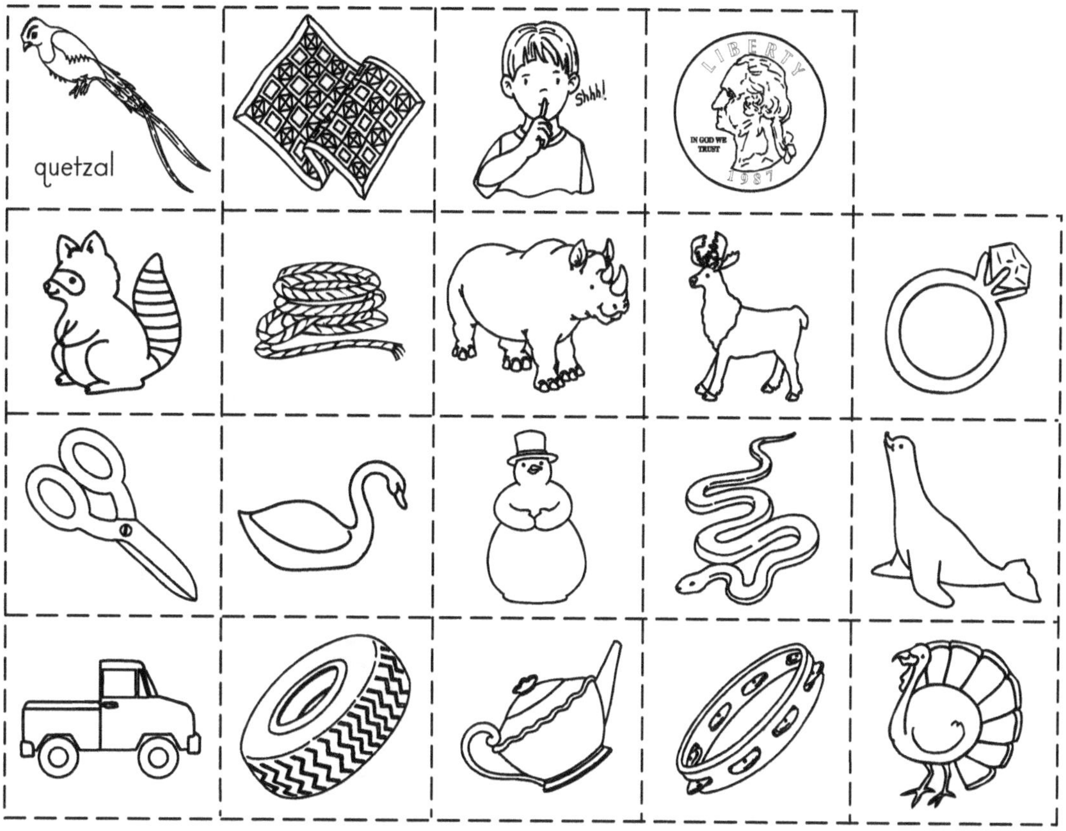

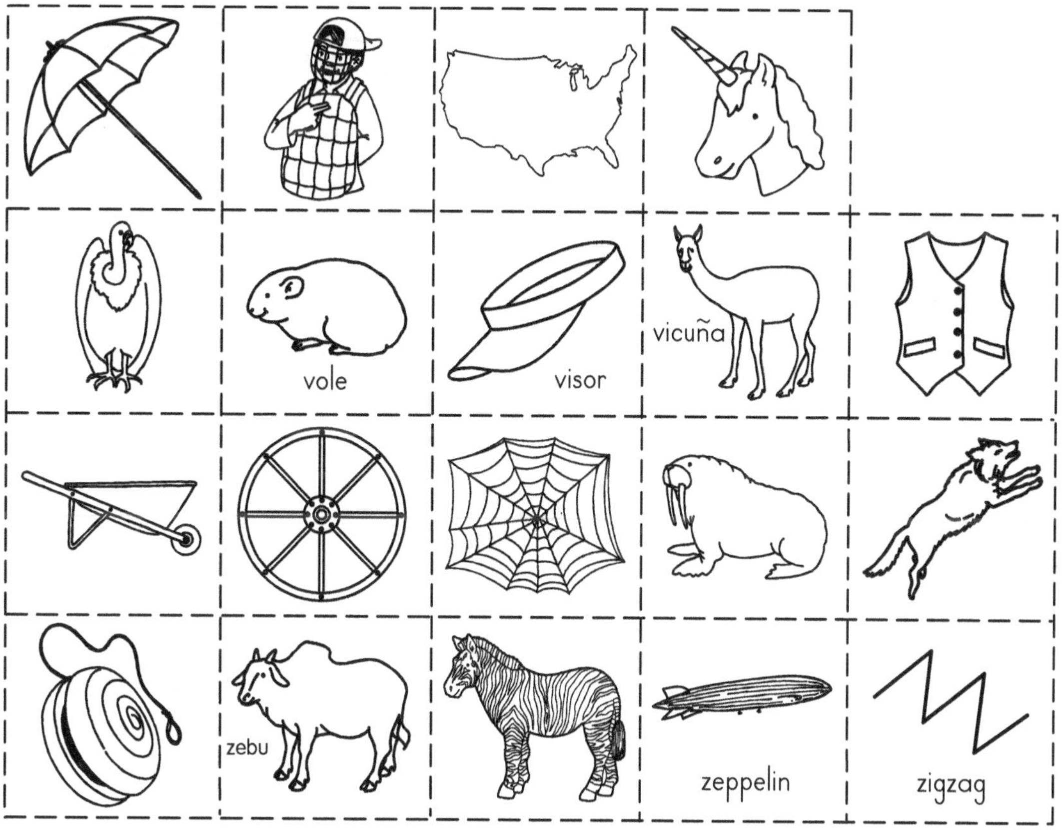

My Alphabet Portfolio Cover

My Alphabet Portfolio

Name _____

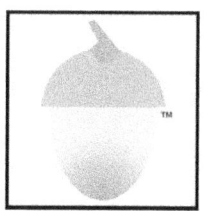

Little Acorn Books™

Promoting Early Skills for a Lifetime™

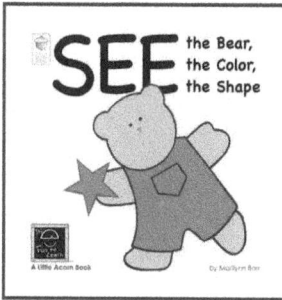   

A Hands-on Picture Book Series Designed to Foster Early Skills • Infancy–Age 4

Using Crayons, Scissors, & Glue for Crafts
Preschool–Grade 1

Miss Pitty Pat & Friends
Preschool–Grade 1

Mookie's Christmas Tree
Not Just for Christmas

Hands-On ABCs • ABC and Readiness Skills Practice for Early Learners

LAB20142P • ABC SCISSOR SKILLS • 978-1-937257-58-3 • © 2014 Little Acorn Books™

www.ingramcontent.com/pod-product-compliance
Lightning Source LLC
Chambersburg PA
CBHW081020040426
42444CB00014B/3288